A Self-Study Course in Official Script

Compiled and written by Huang Quanxin

SINOLINGUA
BEIJING

First Edition   1998

ISBN 7-80052-455-8

Copyright 1998 by Sinolingua

Published by Sinolingua

24 Baiwanzhuang Road, Beijing 100037, China

Printed by Chunlei Printing House

Distributed by China International

Book Trading Corporation

35 Chegongzhuang Xilu, P.O. Box 399

Beijing 100044, China

Printed in the People's Republic of China

Foreword

Chinese calligraphy, the core of the Oriental arts, reflects the temperament of the Chinese nation. The black and white, dots and lines are an expression of the spirits and images of Nature, reflecting a calligrapher's feelings and knowledge. Calligraphy's profound artistic essence lies in the combination of feeling and rationale, form and spirit, rich structure and vivid rhythm – a perfect balance between the form and the ideological content expressed in a character. Though devoid of color, calligraphy is variously colored as painting; and without sound, it contains melodies just like music.

Chinese calligraphy has a long history, ranging from the keeping of records by tying knots before Cang Jie invented writing, to the characters on earthenware discovered at Dawenkou and inscriptions on bones or tortoise shells of the Shang Dynasty (c. 16th-11th century BC). Like a long running river, Chinese calligraphy has evolved during thousands of years, characterized by simplicity and unsophistication in the Shang and Zhou dynasties (c. 16th century-221 BC), splendor in the Qin and Han dynasties (221 BC-AD 220), graceful bearing in the Wei and Jin dynasties (220-420), magnificence in the Sui and Tang dynasties (581-907), radiating vigor in the Song and Yuan dynasties (960-1368), prosperity in the Ming and Qing dynasties (1368-1911) and grandeur in the current era.

Chinese characters fall into the following styles: regular, running, grass, official and seal scripts. Seal scripts may be divided into large and small characters; official scripts, into Qin and Han styles; grass characters, into *Zhang* (cursive official), *Jin* (modern) and *Kuang* (wild) scripts; and regular characters, into Wei and Tang scripts. Chinese calligraphy not only reflects the character of individual calligrapher, but also presents the styles and flavors of different regions and eras.

China has always regarded calligraphy as the quintessence of Chinese culture and a national treasure as well. Calligraphy is a required course at school and every educated person must study calligraphy.

The art of Chinese calligraphy is unprecedentedly prosperous now. Various kinds of calligraphy model books have been published; however, it is hard to find one which can scientifically instruct people in learning calligraphy. An old saying goes: ``If one owns the best book, one may obtain medium-level knowledge; and if one has a medium-level book, one may only absorb low-level knowledge." Anyone who wishes to have a good command of Chinese calligraphy must have a good teacher and a good book. At the present time when it is hard to find a good teacher, good teaching materials are even more important.

To meet the demands of the people who are interested in Chinese calligraphy, Professor Huang Quanxin has compiled the *Chinese Calligraphy Teach-Yourself Series* in six books: *A Self-Study Course in Regular Script, A Self-Study Course in Wei Stone Inscriptions, A Self-Study Course in Running Script, A Self-Study Course in Grass Script, A Self-Study Course in Official Script,* and *A Self-Study Course in Seal Script*. Each book consists of the following chapters: A Brief Introduction, Techniques, Strokes, Radicals, Structure, The Art of Composition, Creation, Copying, and Appreciation, which should help beginners learn the rudiments, and other learners improve their calligraphy techniques.

With standard model characters, systematic theories for self-study, illustration and texts, the *Chinese Calligraphy Teach-Yourself Series* is well formatted, informative and interesting. Student may appreciate Chinese calligraphy while practicing the models in the books to improve their accomplishments and techniques. We sincerely wish they are of help with the study of Chinese calligraphy.

Editor
October 1994

About the Author

Huang Quanxin is a senior teacher of fine arts in the Middle School Attached to Beijing Normal University and a member of the Chinese Calligraphers' Association. In his childhood, he took up the study of calligraphy and paintings, and read a large number of poems. His father was a student of Kang Youwei (a famous reformist in the late Qing Dynasty). For many years, he has lived in Liulichang (an ancient cultural street in Beijing), taken many famous calligraphers, scholars and experts as his teachers, and immersed himself untiringly among calligraphy and painting. When he was a middle-school student, he won first place in a calligraphy contest. Later many more works won awards at important calligraphy competitions and have been exhibited at home and abroad. In addition, he has inscribed the titles of many newspapers and magazines. He is named as an eminent person of the contemporary era by the Calligraphy Association of Wang Xizhi's hometown, included in the book *Famous Calligraphers in Beijing* by the Beijing Calligraphers' Association, as well as in *A Dictionary of Chinese Artists of the Present Age* and *Who's Who in the World*.

Huang Quanxin is also a member of the Chinese Society for Fine Arts Education and a standing council member of the district society. In his youth, he compiled teaching materials for the fine arts, painted color picture-story books, and created hanging paintings, which were named by the State Education Commission as excellent works. He visited Taiwan as a member of the artists delegation from mainland China and held a one-man calligraphy show in Japan. Many of his calligraphy works and paintings have been sent by the government officials to foreign guests as gifts, enjoying a high reputation both at home and abroad. Hence he is included in the book *Famous Chinese Painters*.

Huang Quanxin has served as teacher for thirty years, with students from all over the country and some in foreign countries. Quite a number of his students came out top at many domestic and international calligraphy and paintings competitions.

Huang Quanxin founded the first parents' school in Beijing and has served as head of the National Excellent Parents' School for many years. He is a consultant of Beijing primary and middle-school education, a former host of an education program of Beijing Broadcasting Station, one of the compilers of the teaching materials and courses of the Beijing Parents' School, a member of the Beijing Research Association of Family Education and a council member of the district research association. He is also interested in various aspects of Chinese traditional culture and arts, and serves as a council member of the Association for Developing Beijing and Kunqu Operas.

Huang Quanxin has devoted his spare time to the study of calligraphy, paintings and other Chinese traditional culture and arts as well as to the education of arts. Up to now more than thirty of his books have been published, including *Grand View of China's Auspiciousness Series*, *The Series of Authentic Characters of Fu (fortune), Lu (emoluments), Shou (longevity) and Xi (happiness) by Famous Calligraphers of Past Dynasties*, *Modern Inscriptions*, *A Copybook of Ancient Chinese Poems*, *An Intense Course for Practical Fountain Pen Handwriting*, and *Elementary Handwriting for Young People*. In addition he has been a designer for many books. Huang Quanxin, who enjoys a high reputation in China and abroad, is included in the *Directory of Eminent Literary Personnel of China* by the Research Institute of Literature of the China Academy of Social Sciences.

Contents

Chapter I   Official Script

1. Origin and Development

Official script, which derived from seal characters, was in the bud in the Warring States Period (475-221 BC), came into being in the Qin Dynasty (221-207 BC), developed in the Western Han (206 BC-24) and reached its prime in the Eastern Han (25-220).

The appearance of official script was an important reform in the history of the Chinese characters and calligraphy, which led to the modern form of Chinese writing. Grass characters, running and regular scripts all evolved from official script. Hence official script is the origin of present-day Chinese characters.

2. Qin Official Script

Qin official script is also known as ancient official script. In the Qin Dynasty, though small seal characters were designated for use in official and governmental documents, a cursive, swiftly-written and simplified form of seal characters, later known as official scripts, was widely used among the people.

Qin official script is similar to seal characters in structure, but it differs from seal characters in the strokes. As official script stressed convenience and speed, curving lines in seal characters were replaced by straight lines in Qin official script; and round cornering strokes, by square cornering ones. These are the most important differences between Qin official script and small seal characters.

3. Simplified Han Official Script

The official script in the Western Han Dynasty was represented by simplified Han official script. Qin official script is the cursive form of small seal characters, and in many respects remains the overall form. In spite of the influence of seal characters, official script developed quickly in the Western Han. Highlighted by simplified and neatened character structure and reformed character composition, official script, instead of small seal characters, became commonly used for writing in the Western Han Dynasty.

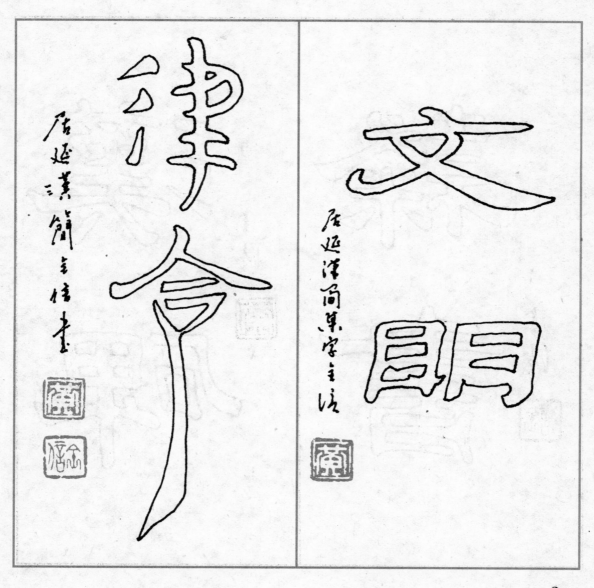

4. Han Official Script

Gradually the writing of official script became an art in the later Western Han Dynasty. All horizontal, left-falling and right-falling strokes show a rising trend, the end of a stroke becomes thick and the closing of a stroke is slightly lifted up. The Eastern Han Dynasty witnessed the appearance of a large number of stone inscriptions and official script reached its height. Each stone inscription displays its own distinct style. Some were simple and unsophisticated; some, square and beautiful; and others, elegant and graceful.

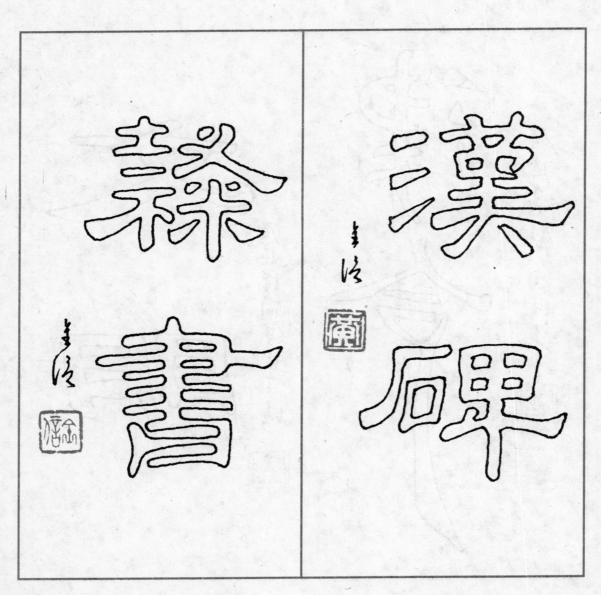

Chapter II   Techniques of Writing

1. Sitting Position

Requirements for one who sits to write:

The head: One should hold the head straight, inclined slightly forward, look at the copybook and keep the mind peaceful.

The body: One should sit straight, keep the shoulders level and the waist stiff, and should not touch the table with the chest.

The arms: One should relax one's arms, the left hand resting on the paper and the right hand holding the brush.

The feet: One should rest one's feet parallel on the floor, the legs relaxed and the body stable.

2. Standing Position

One should stand to write large Chinese characters, with a suspended elbow.

Hold the head straight, incline the body slightly forward, look at the copybook and keep the mind peaceful.

Hold the brush with the right hand, place the left hand on the table, and suspend the elbow while writing characters to freely express one's feeling.

Place the right foot slightly forward and the left foot slightly back, and rest the soles flat on the floor with the center of gravity on the right foot.

Write characters with the strength from the waist and the roots of the feet to make every stroke penetrate the paper.

3. Holding the Brush

Hold the brush straight with fingers, the palm relaxed.

Pushing down: The thumb pushes the brush from inside to outside.

Pressing: The index finger presses the brush from outside to inside.

Hooking: The middle finger pulls the brush from outside on the left to inside on the right.

Squaring: The ring finger pushes the brush from inside on the right to outside on the left.

Supporting: The little finger gives auxiliary strength to the ring finger.

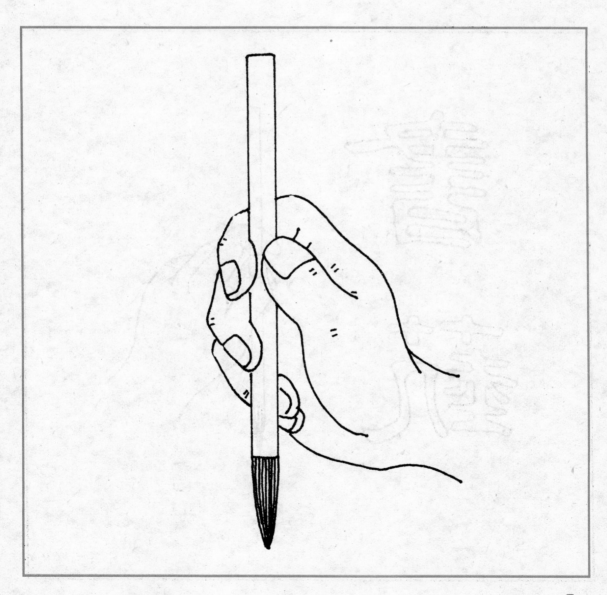

4. Movement of the Brush

A saying goes: Moving the brush with the wrist. If the middle point of the brush is used in the movement of the brush, all strength will be concentrated on the writing brush and strokes will be full of spirit. One should use the contrary-point method to start a stroke; the middle-point method, to move the brush on; and the hidden-point method to close a stroke.

The "swallow-tail" right falling stroke is particular to official script. With a round beginning like a silkworm's head and a square end in the shape of a swallow's tail, the curving right falling stroke is vivid, like flowing water. There are little changes in the other strokes of official script.

Chapter III   Strokes

The single movement of the brush is commonly known as one stroke. One who wants to write good calligraphy must learn to write strokes well.

1. Basic Strokes

There are eight kinds of basic strokes: horizontal, vertical, left-falling, right-falling, hooking, rising and cornering strokes and dots.

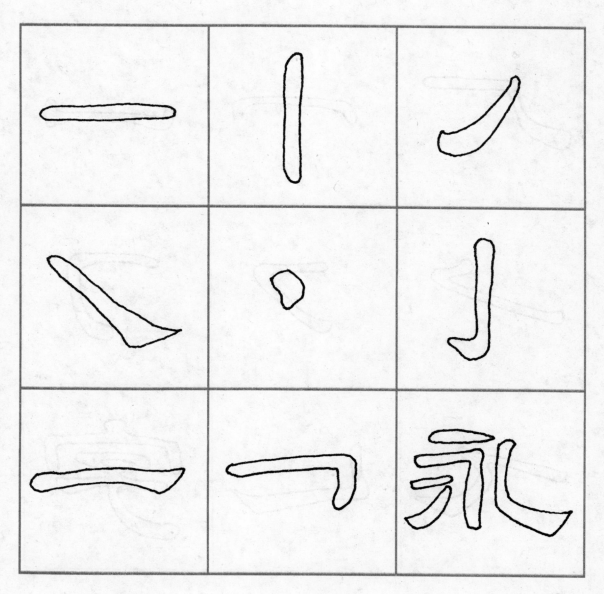

2. Complex Strokes

The strokes in the Chinese calligraphy are divided into basic strokes and complex strokes. A complex stroke consists of two to three basic strokes. There are eight kinds of basic strokes and tens kinds of complex strokes.

After one has learnt how to write the basic strokes, one should continue to practise complex strokes, which are also basic skills for calligraphy.

The following are eight kinds of complex strokes.

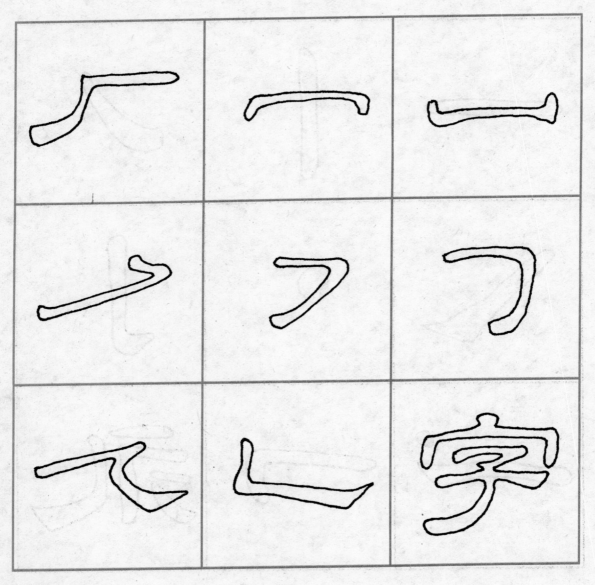

3. The Changes of Strokes

Different horizontal strokes	王	主
言	三	朝
宰	宰	長
奉	泰	請

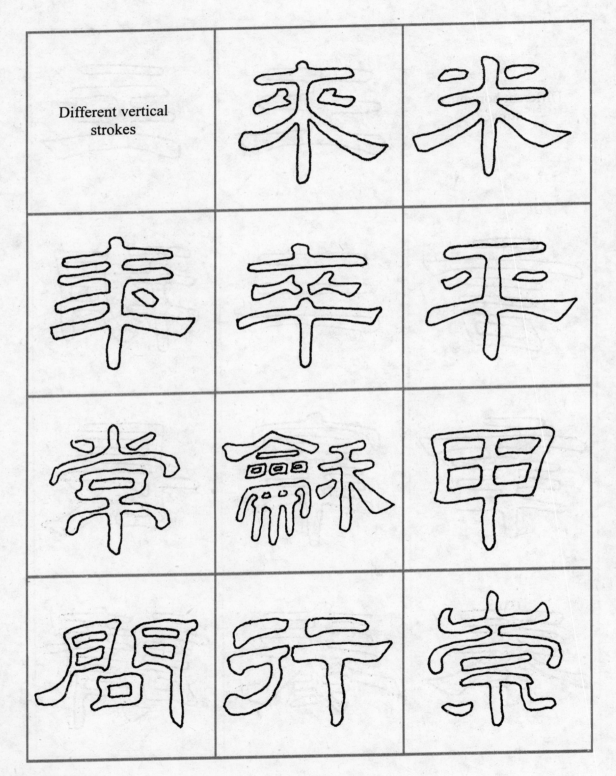

Different vertical
strokes

Different left-falling strokes

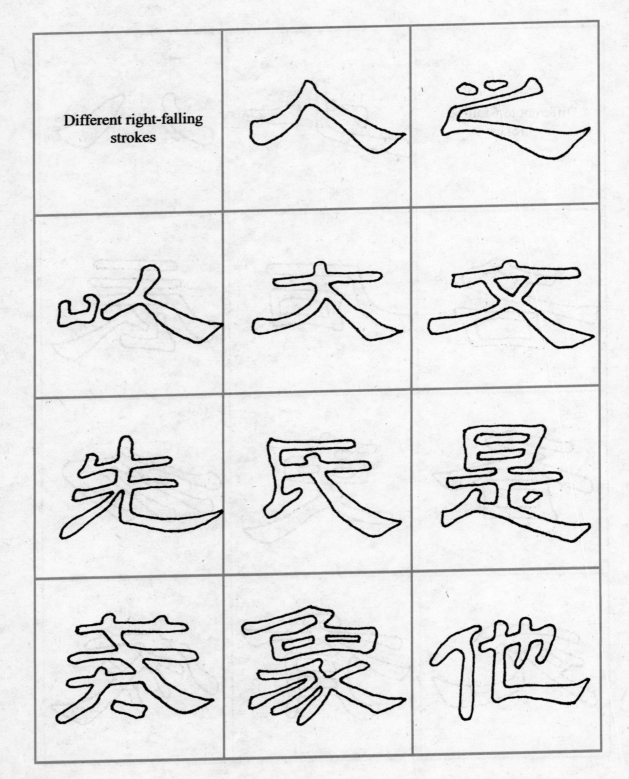

Different right-falling strokes

Different hooking strokes	于	手
子	可	弘
守	川	恰
状	祠	特

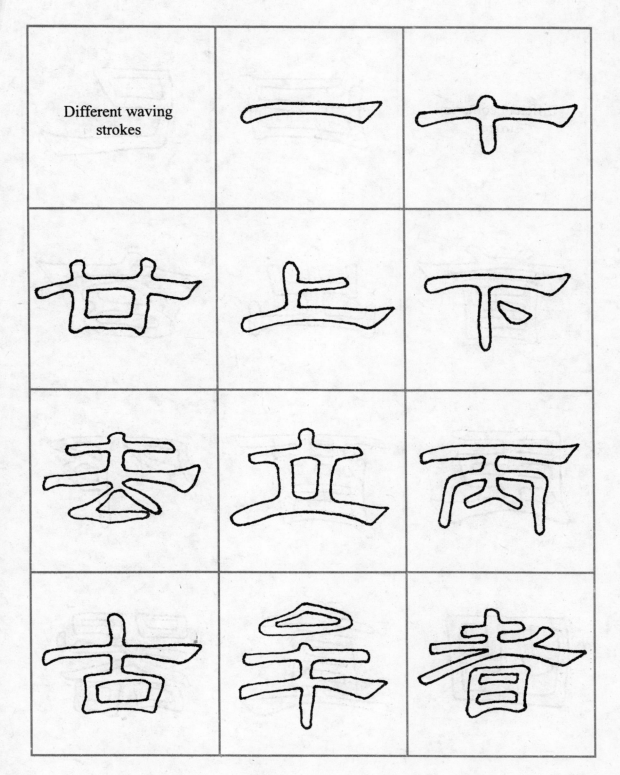

Different waving strokes

一 十 廿 上 下 去 立 丙 古 羊 者

Different cornering strokes

4. The Order of Strokes

First horizontal, then vertical	一	元
元	亚	平
一	二	三
示	三	秉

First left-falling, then right-falling	丿	勹
口	史	史
一	丆	又
尽	各	各

First top, then bottom	一	二
屮	牛	先
一	コ	ク
尹	君	君

First left, then right	ゝ	力
力	加	加口
ヽ	ニ	ラ
ラ一	ラ二	行

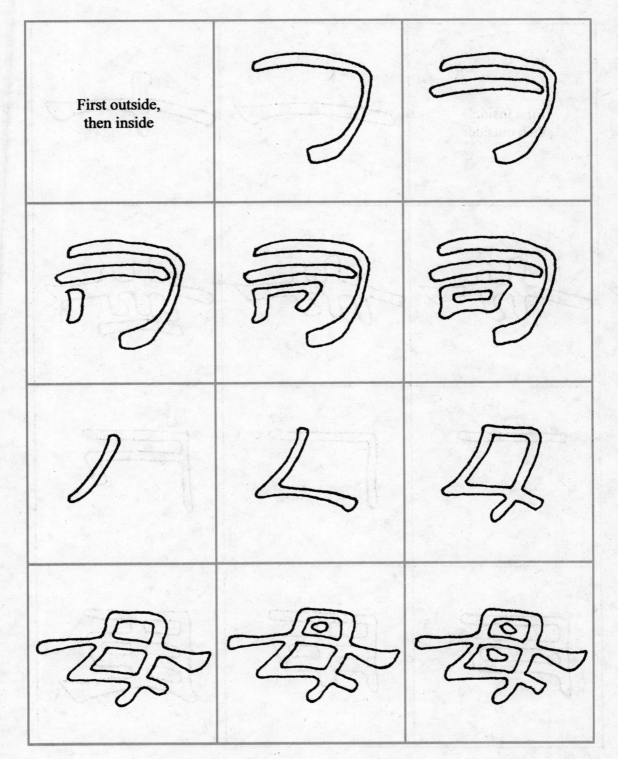

First outside,
then inside

First inside,
then outside

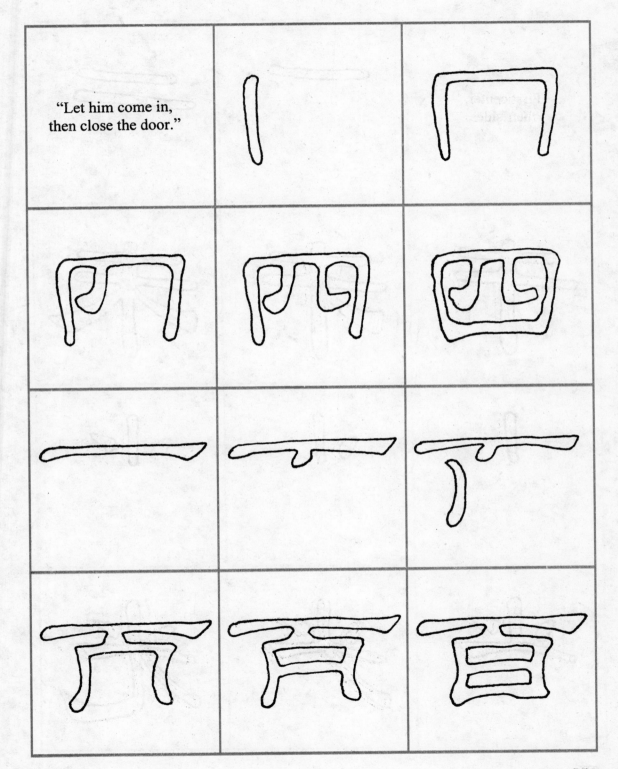

"Let him come in,
then close the door."

First center, then sides	一	二
十	末	未
丨	小	小
屮	光	光

Chapter IV   Radicals

Side components are the main parts composing compound-element characters. The characters with the same side component belong to the same radical.

More than 90 percent of the Chinese characters are compound-element characters. The number of the characters with the same side component varies from several dozens to several hundred. For instance, there are nearly 600 Chinese characters with the side component of 氵. So if one can write one side component well, it will help in writing well many Chinese characters with the same side component.

The radicals are divided into the character's head, character's bottom, left component, right component and character's frame.

1. Character's Head

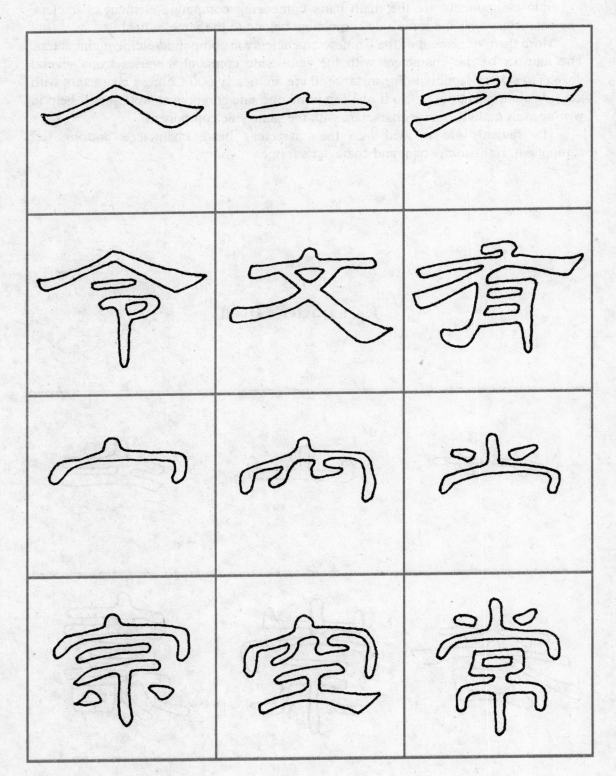

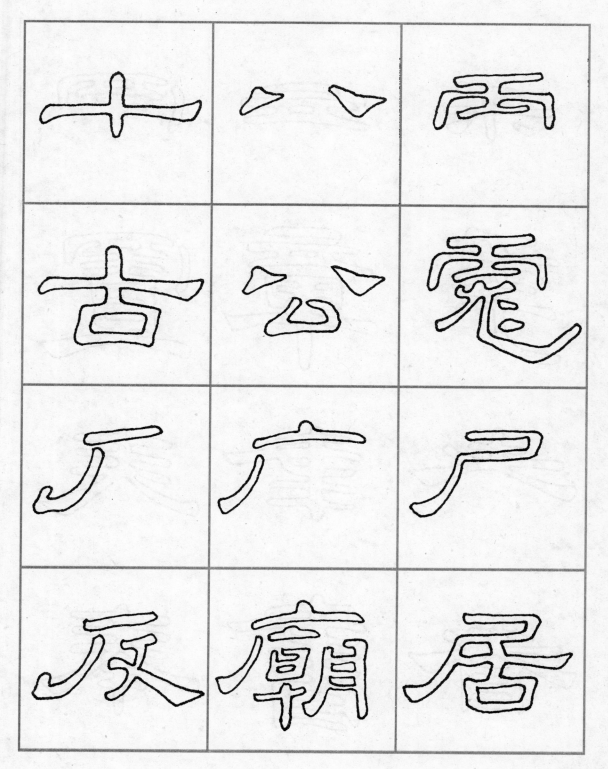

示	金	雨
季	章	置
大	車	美
者	書	奉

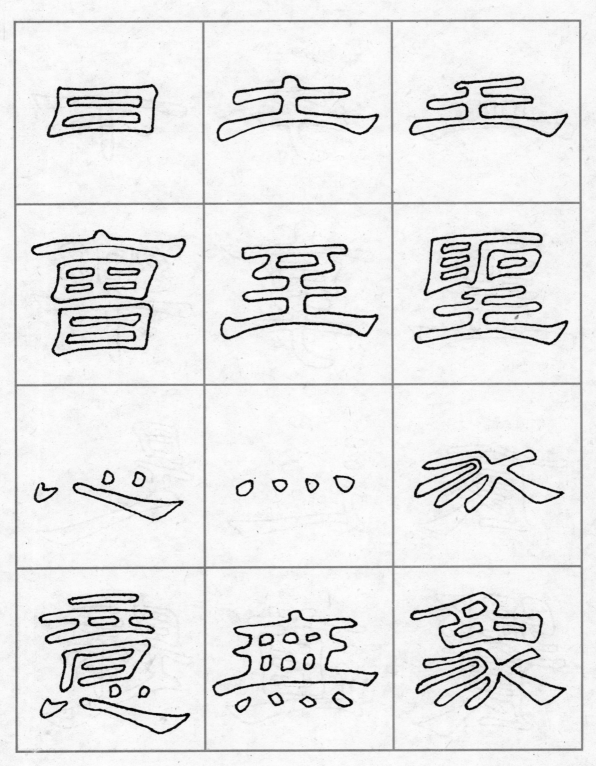

皿	字	亦
盡	享	樂
夏	之	是
響	道	歸

3. Left Component

二	三	阝
馮	河	除
彳	弓	女
伯	行	始

朮	禾	禾
相	秋	神
才	予	屮
揫	孔	皇

土	王	弓
地	瑛	弘
絫	米	衣
給	精	補

牛	魚	馬
牛特	魚鮑	馬騎
弓	季	足
狀	報	跟

口	立	金
吹	端	錢
音	方	食
韻	於	餘

4. Right Component

寸	寸	攴
利	尉	歌
又	攵	力
叙	故	功

卩	阝	月
即	郭	朝
飪	罕	頁
雒	霏	頭

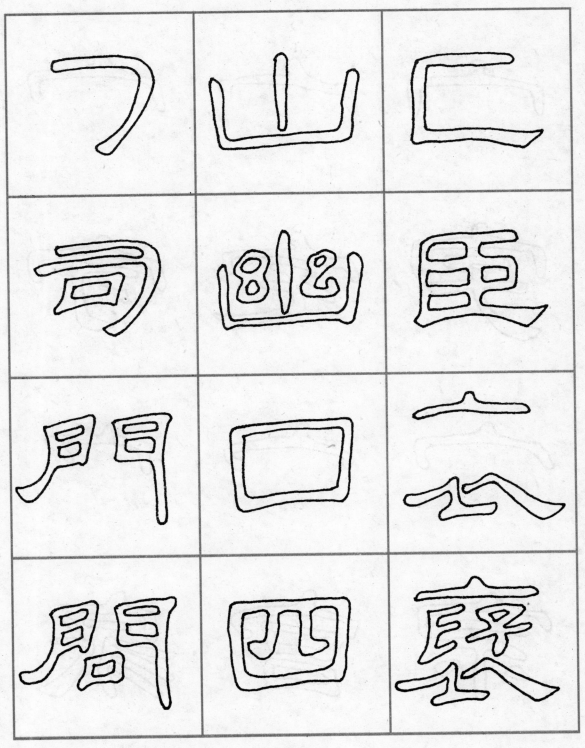

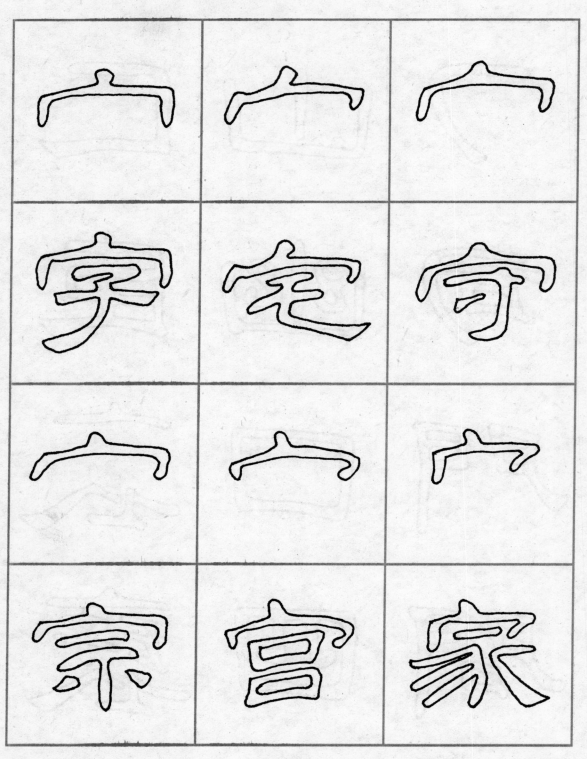

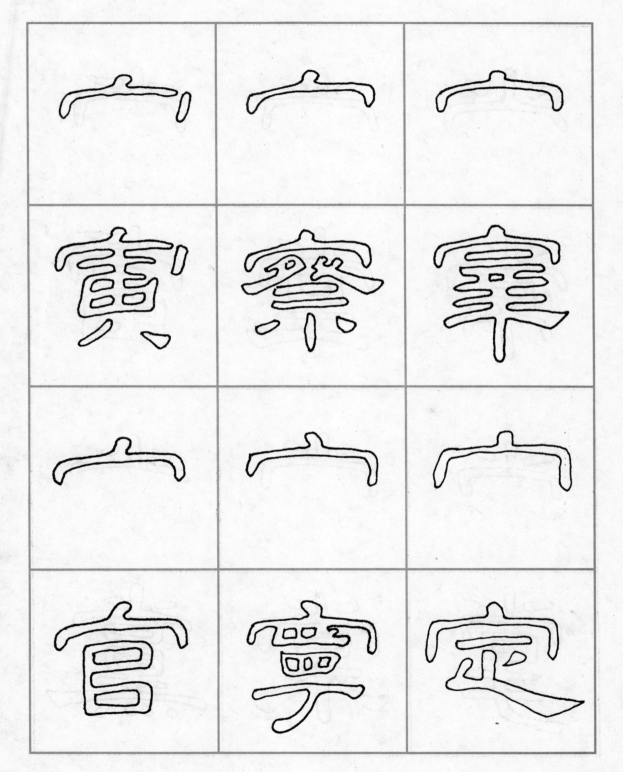

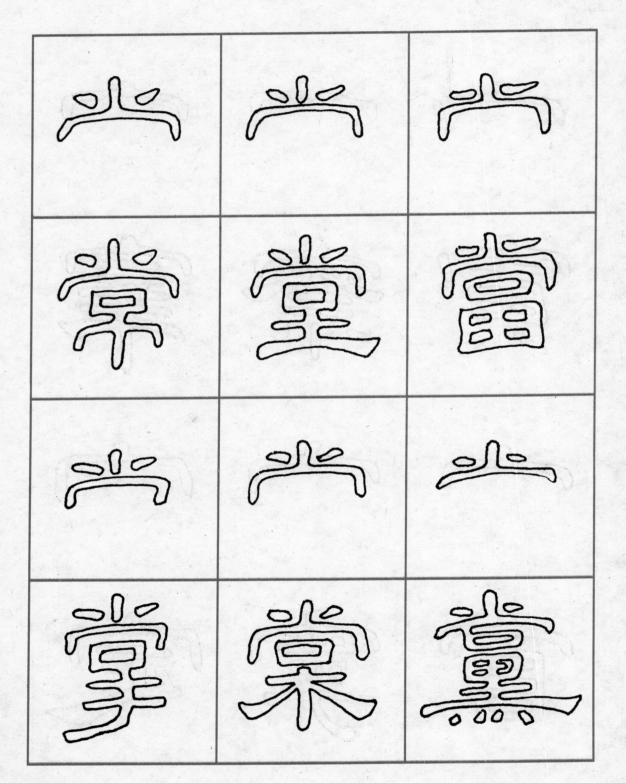

艸 艸

艸 艸

艸 艸

芏 若 萬

艸 艸

艸 艸

艸 艸

節 蕩 等

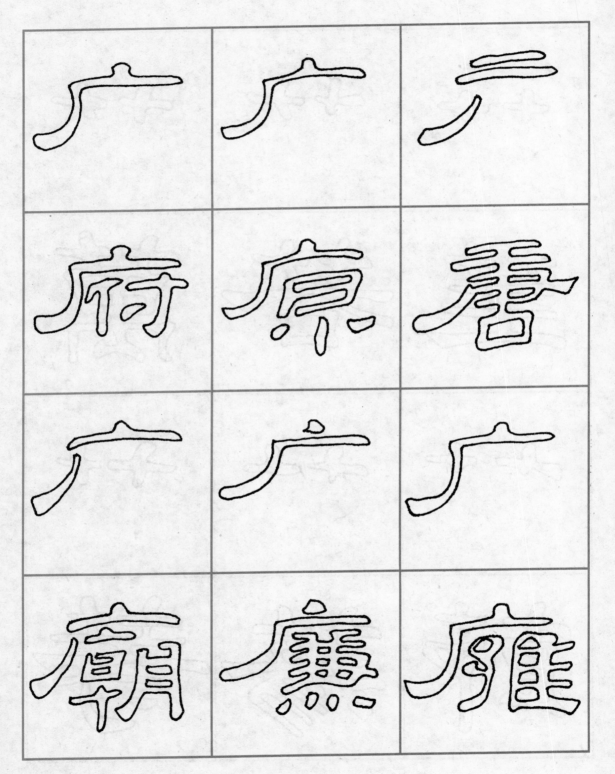

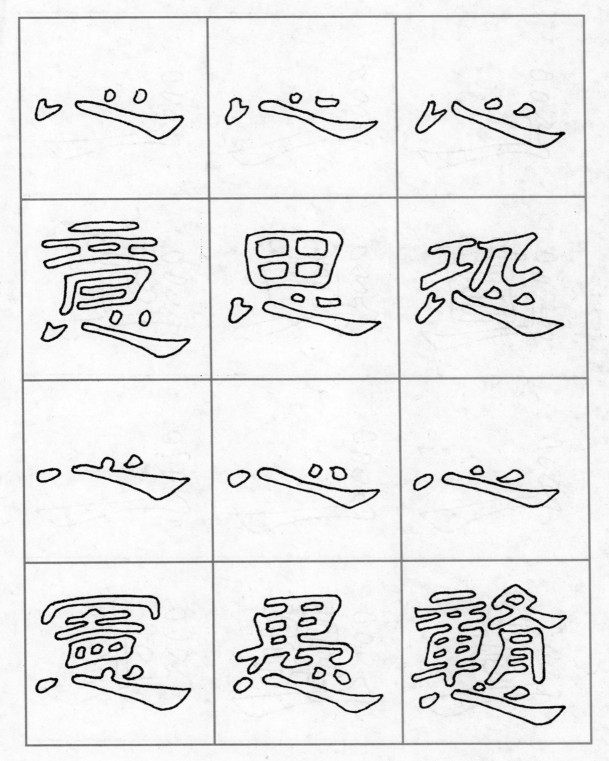

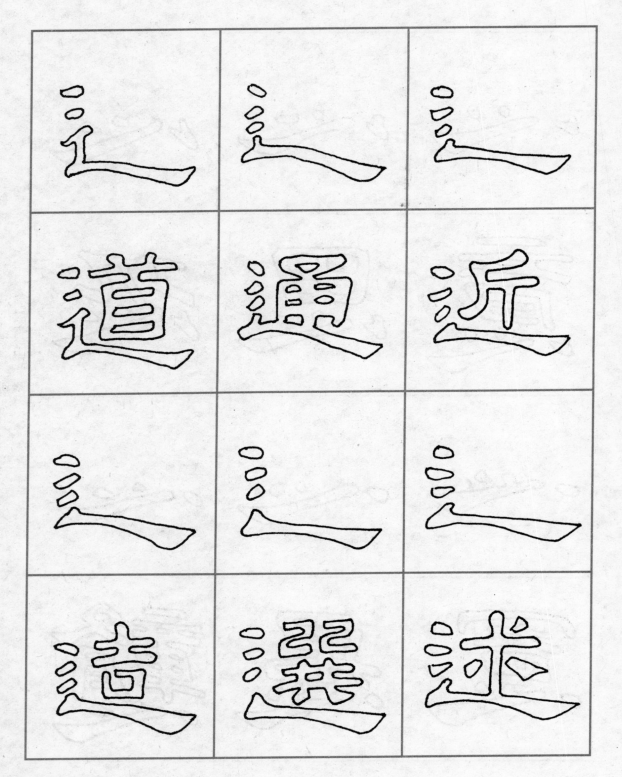

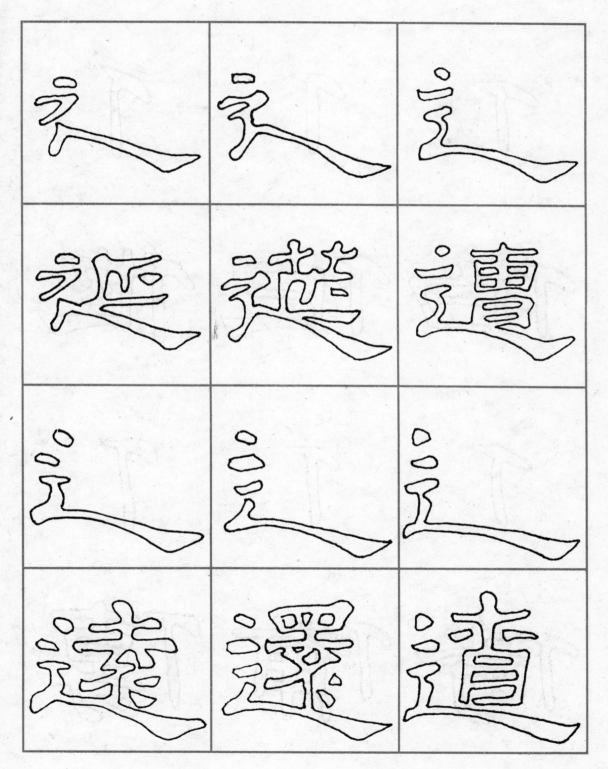

亻	亻	亻
佰	佐	他
丁	丁	丁
侍	備	傳

亻　　亻　　亻

僃　　俯　　仰

亻　　亻　　亻

億　　僚　　侵

亻	亻	亻
代	仲	化
亻	亻	亻
伏	佐	俾

氵	氵	氵
江	计	決
氵	氵	氵
池	浑	瀆

氵	三	氵
河	酒	頁
氵	氵	氵
演	漢	隹

ヲ	ヲ	テ
ヲ行	ヲ徒	テ芷
ヲ	ヲ	ヲ
ヲ癔	ヲ津	ヲ後

才	才	才
揣	持	挂
才	才	才
援	撰	攝

示	示	示
祝	神	祠
示	示	示
祀	禔	禮

言　言　言

許　讀　詒

言　言　言

誠　謹　試

才	刁	刊
利	財	刊
刊	刊	才
制	列	到

Chapter V   Structure

Three key points to the Chinese calligraphy are well-written strokes, well-knit structure and vivid spirit.

The frame structure of a Chinese character is called the structure for short. The frame refers to the proportions of all parts of a character; and the structure, the composing rules of strokes.

1. Structural Forms

Generally Chinese characters are classified into eight structural forms: single structure, top-bottom structure, top-middle-bottom structure, left-right structure, left-middle-right structure, semi-closing structure, enclosing structure and 品-character structure.

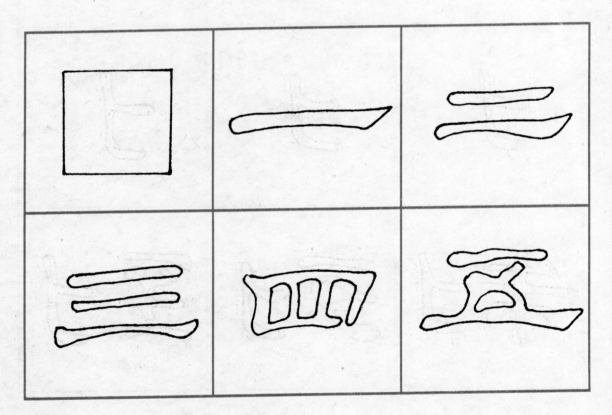

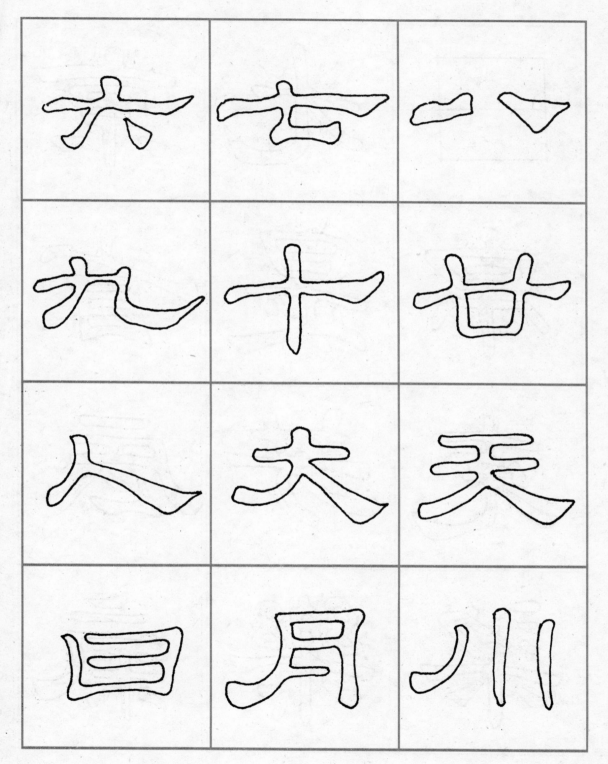

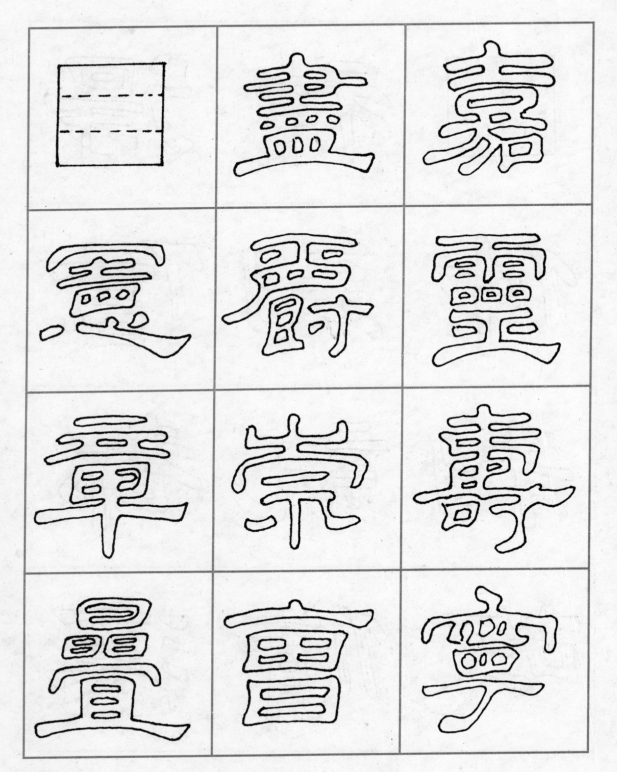

2. Outline of the Structure

Chinese characters developed from the irregularly shaped inscriptions on bones or tortoise shells of the Shang Dynasty (c. 16th-11th century BC), and the later rectangle seal characters to square Han official script. Since then, Chinese characters have been known as block-style characters.

In general, Han official script is slightly deltoid in shape. But many characters have developed into the shapes of a circle, triangle, trapezoid and polygon. Even the square characters vary in sizes.

To understand the outline of the structure will help us know the structure of a character as a whole.

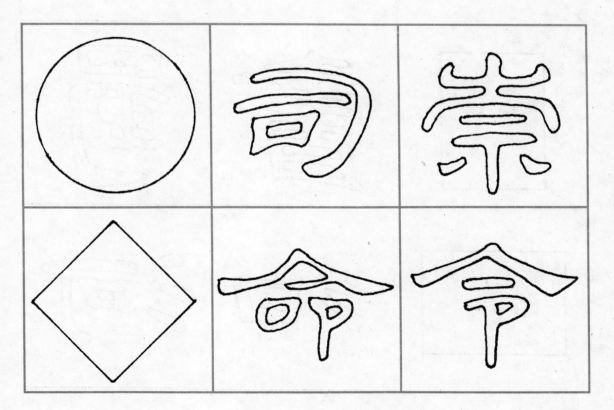

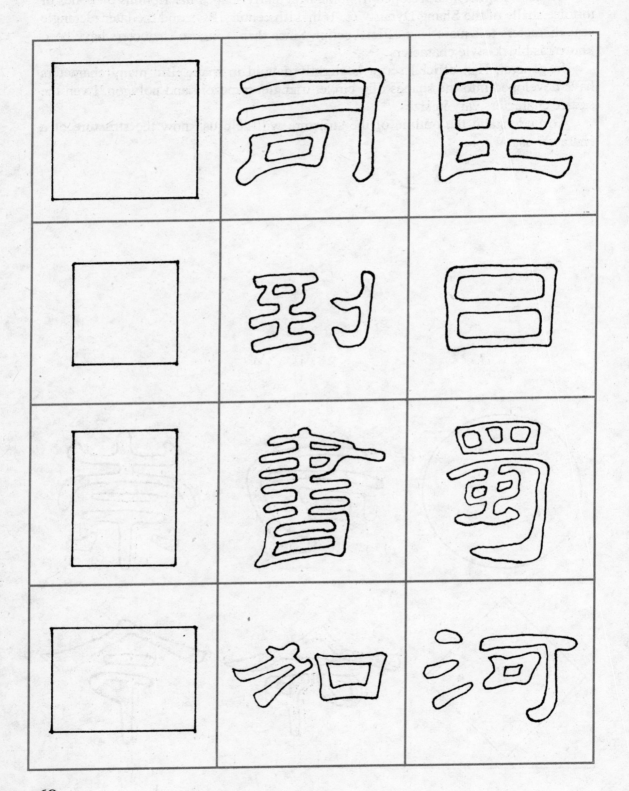

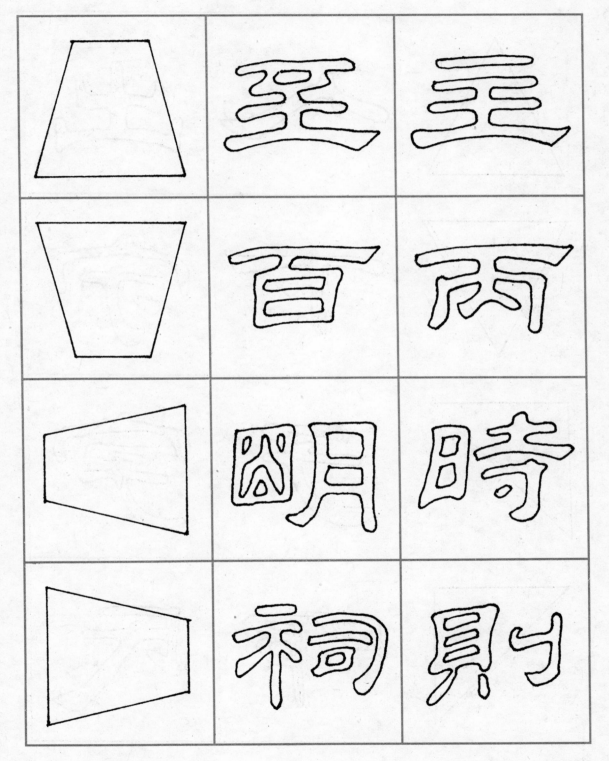

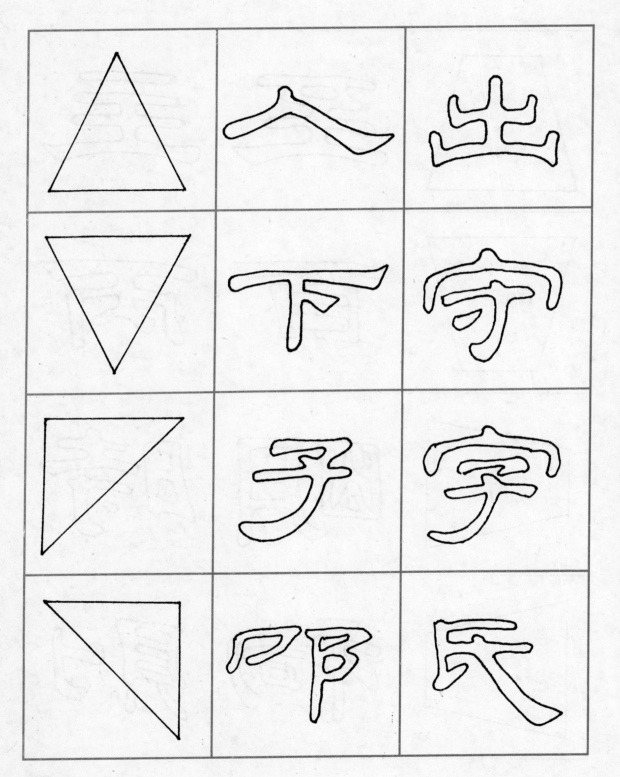

3. The Laws of the Structure

The laws of the structure refer to the conditions one must have, and the rules and principles one must follow, in creating beautifully shaped Chinese characters.

To understand and master the laws of the structure is very important to the study of the structure. One should not only know how the structure of a character is arranged, but also understand why the character is arranged in such a way. In this way one may better master the rules of the structure and cultivate one's ability to create one's own structures, thus reaching a lofty realm.

Each of various schools of Chinese calligraphy has its own characteristics; however, all of them must follow certain "rules". For instance, some structural rules must be abided by.

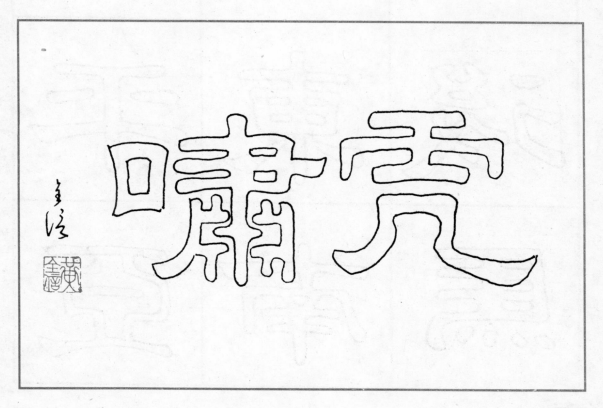

Levelled horizontal strokes; straight vertical strokes; a stable center of gravity; a balanced and dignified shape.	舍	吏
夫	井	史
後	東	平
馬	南	亞

Even density; well-arranged strokes.

An appropriate proportion;
prominent main strokes.

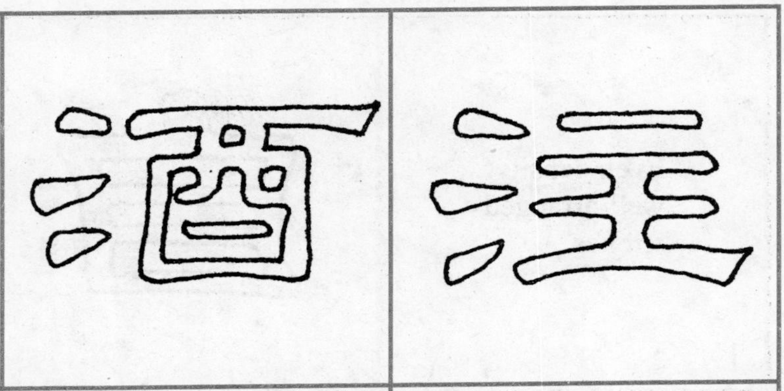

酒　注

桐　泳　寺

補　於　能

優　諫　錢

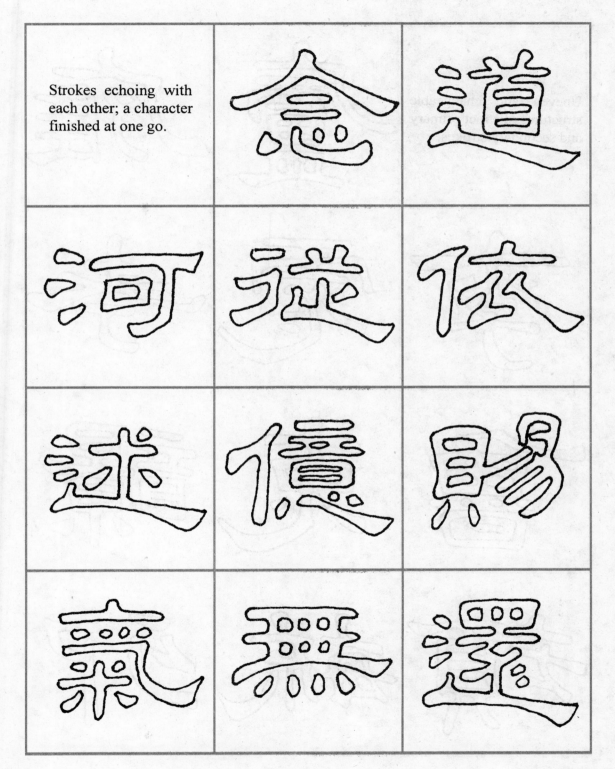

Strokes echoing with each other; a character finished at one go.

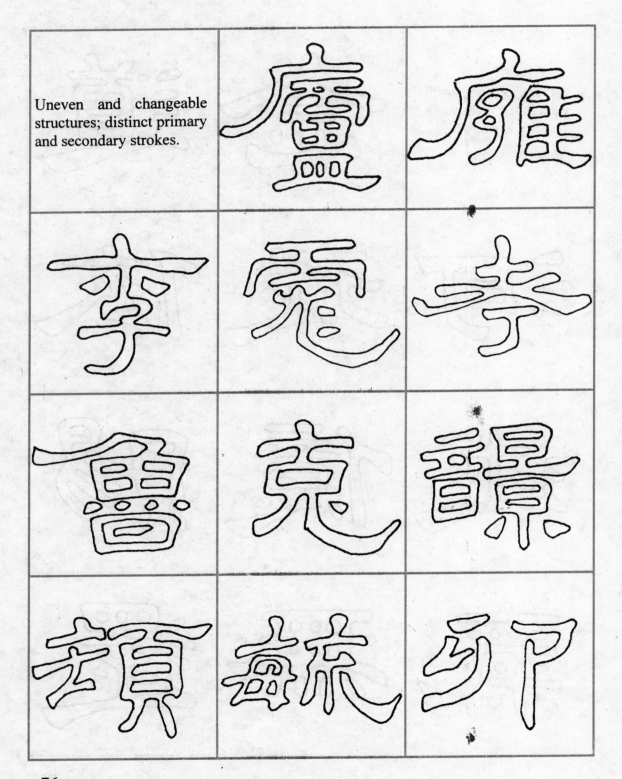

Uneven and changeable structures; distinct primary and secondary strokes.

Coordinated strokes; an even frame; a unified style; a natural shape.	髭	鬣
敬	黑	享
撰	嘗	寰
雖	劉	南

4. The Characteristics of the Structure

Official script characters are squat-shaped, with strokes stretching horizontally to left and right, as compared with seal script featured by elongated strokes. Like "a swallow spreading its wings", official script has a structure of tight inside and lax outside.

Round cornering strokes in seal script are replaced by square cornering strokes in official script; curving lines, by straight lines; and time-consuming writing, by convenient and speedy writing. In addition official script displays coherent and echoing strokes.

The wave-shaped stroke is the most outstanding characteristic of official script, whose "silkworm head" and "swallow's tail" display its unique beauty. The wave-shaped stroke is often the main stroke of a character. Usually, the wave-like stroke appears only once in a character; because "a silkworm does not have two heads" and "no two swallows fly wing to wing".

In addition, other parts of an official-script character stand evenly and independently.

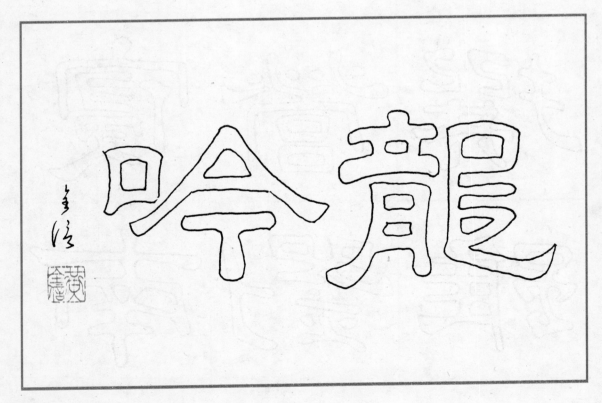

Characters spread horizontally, stretching out to left and right.	大	及
色	各	左
不	所	令
尼	美	水

Square cornering strokes express continuous meaning.

孔　隋

池　治　部

勑　娃　尋

種　屋　顏

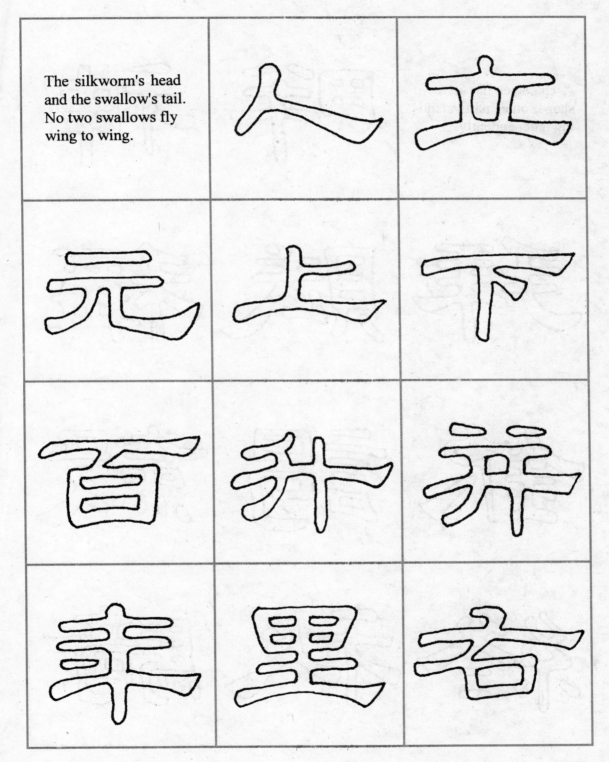

The silkworm's head
and the swallow's tail.
No two swallows fly
wing to wing.

A character has its own shape, other parts standing independently.

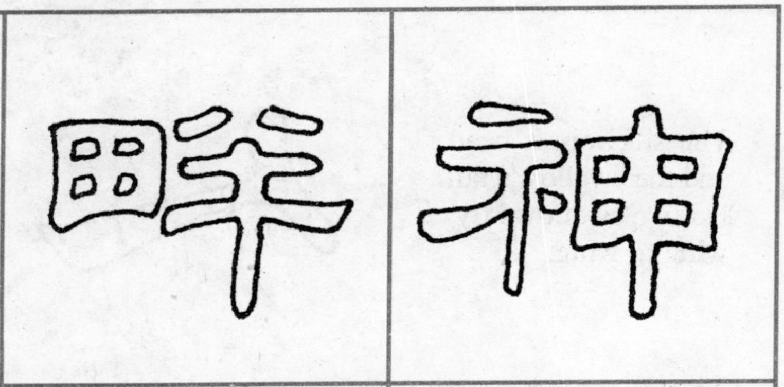

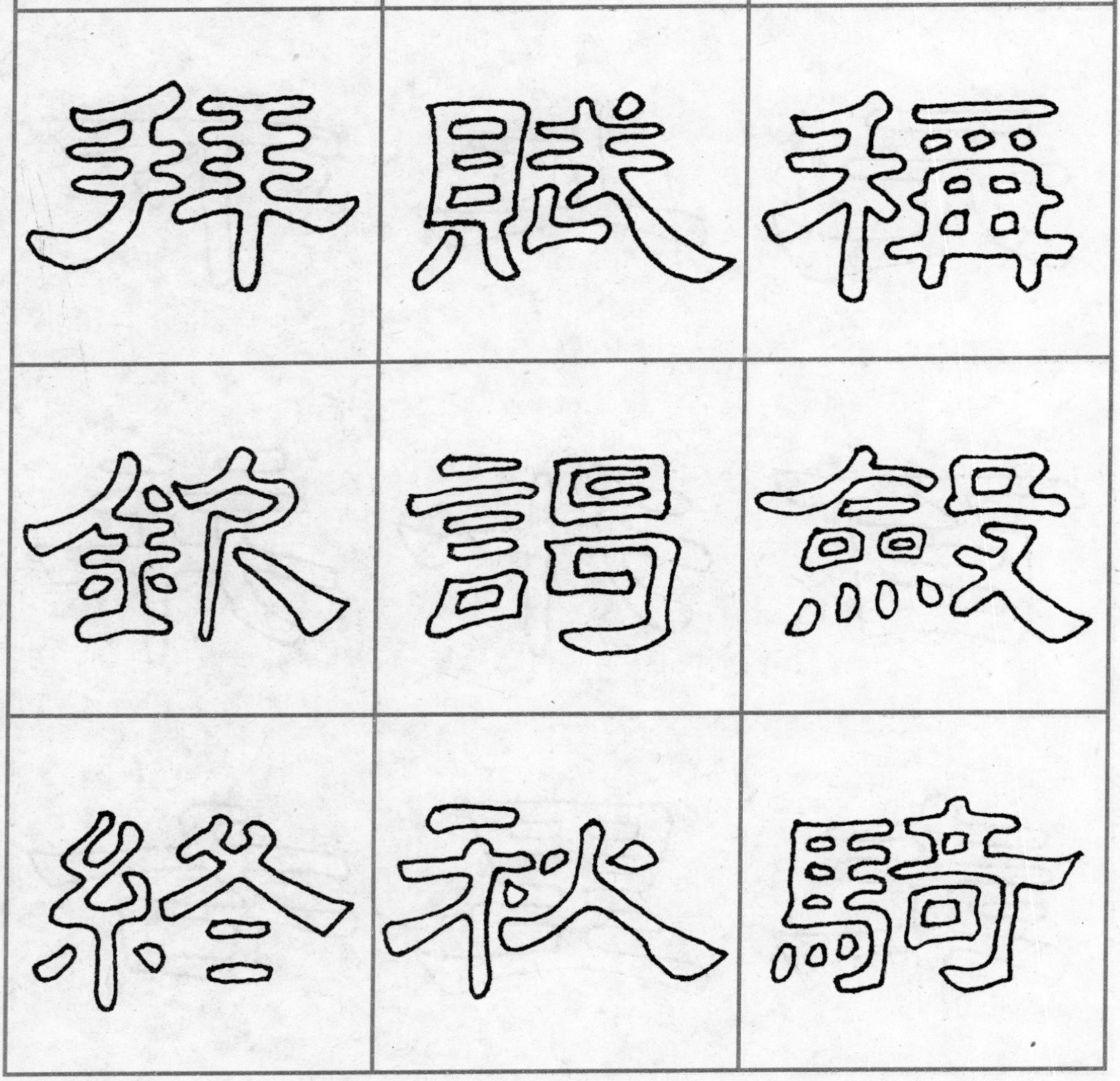

畔 神

拜 賦 稱

欽 謂 毅

終 秋 騎

5. Changes in the Structure

In the *Calligraphy Manual*, Sun Guoting made a brilliant exposition on the diversification and unification of the Chinese calligraphy. He said: "If a character has many strokes, each stroke should show its own distinct style; and all well-arranged strokes should echo each other.... Diversification does not mean to violate the law of the Chinese calligraphy; and unification does not mean to write all characters in a same style."

"Diversification" refers to various, changeable, different, and special parts which consist of an artistic whole, each showing its unique characteristics.

As to a beautiful structure, "diversification" means various different strokes in a common character, showing different and plentiful characteristics.

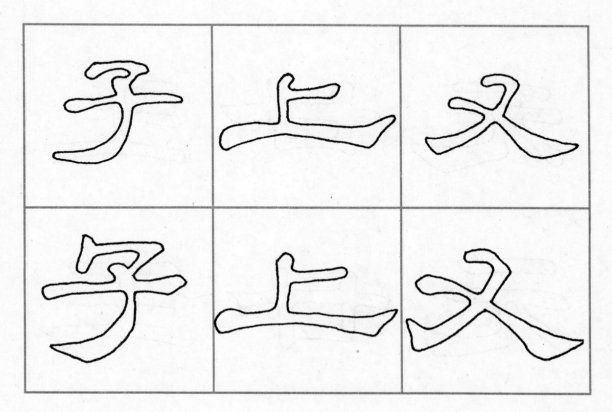

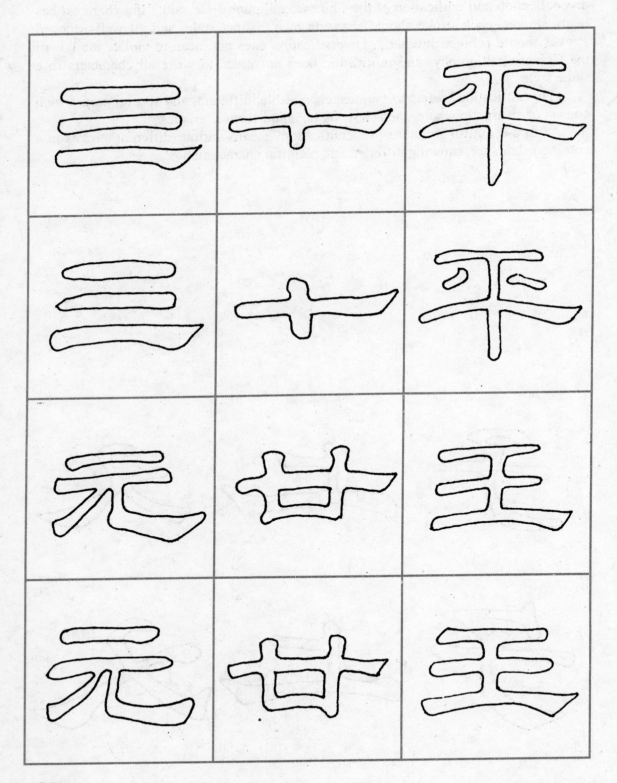

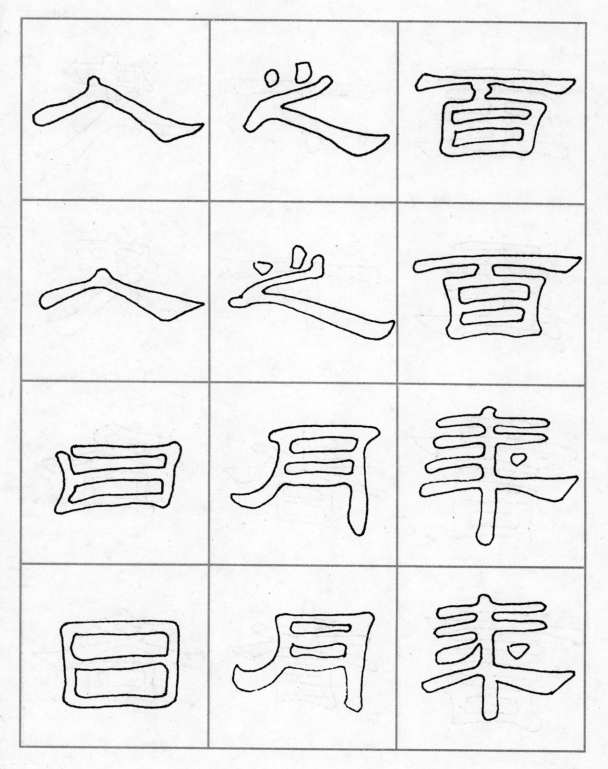

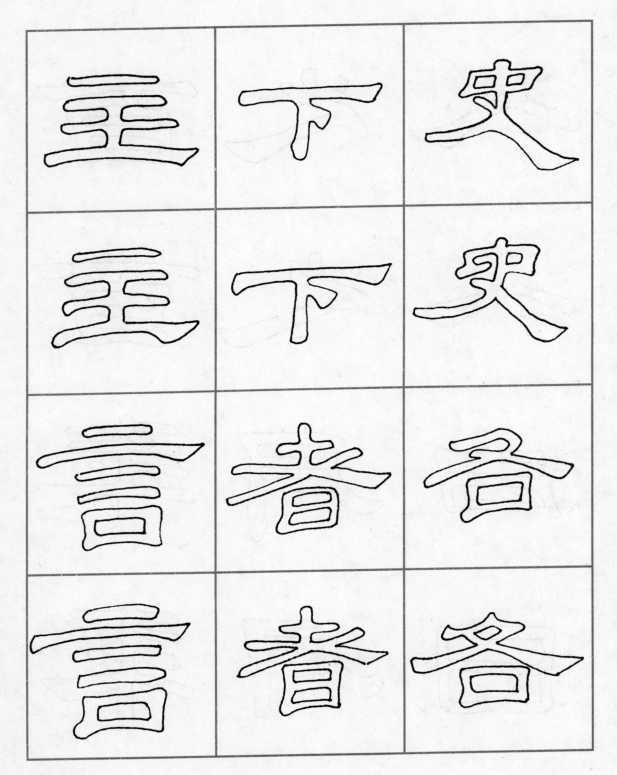

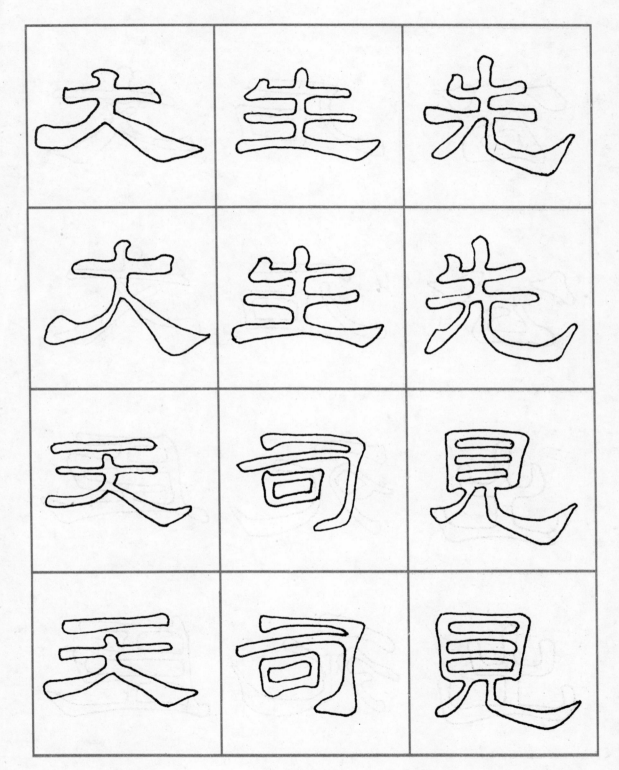

大 生 先
大 生 先
天 司 見
天 司 見

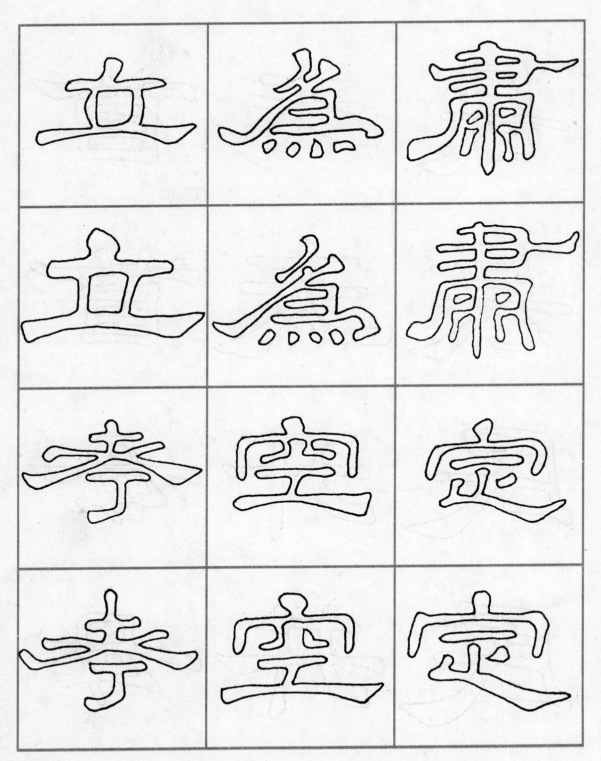

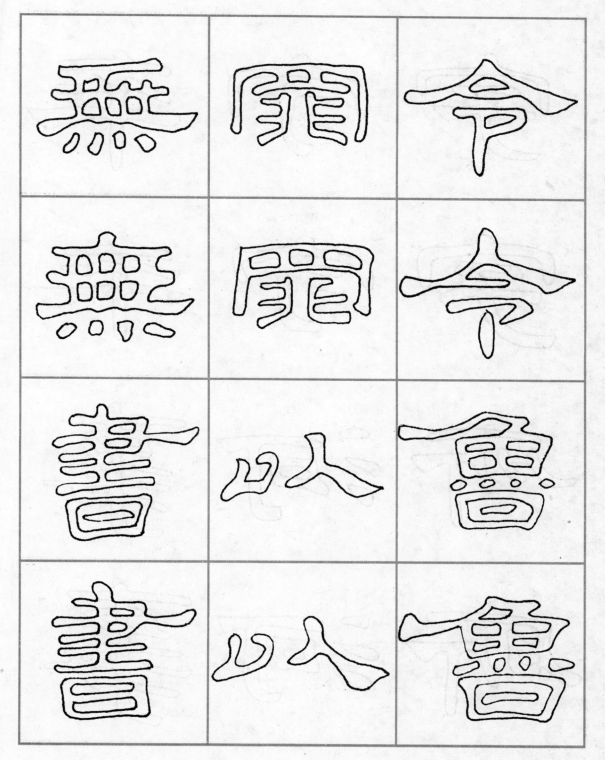

孔	俟	佗
孔	俟	佗
顏	行	制
顏	行	制

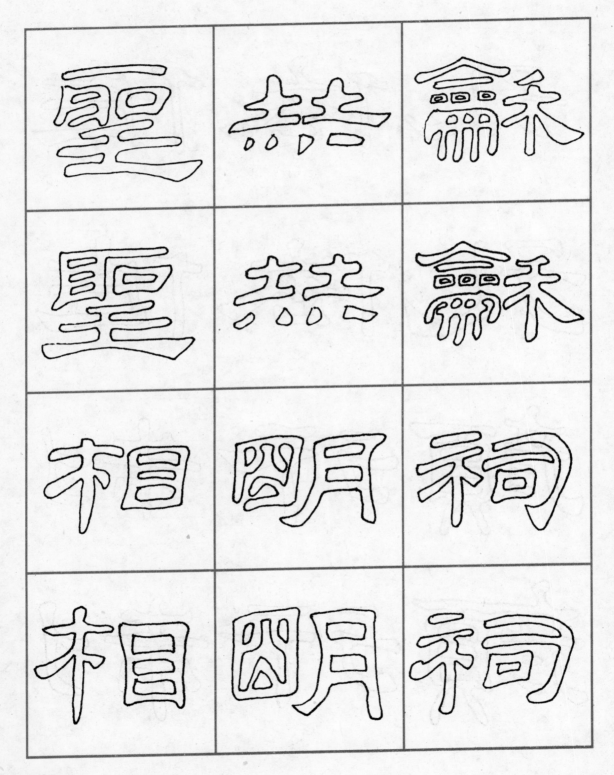

Chapter VI   Tracing and Copying

Tracing and copying are two ways to learn Chinese calligraphy. A beginner should start with tracing and take copying as the mainstay.

Tracing: Place a piece of transparent paper on top of the model and trace it with a brush and ink as exactly as possible.

Copying: Put the model in front of the writer and copy characters as accurately as possible.

There are many ways to copy Chinese characters: line copying, check copying, frame copying, contrasting copying, backing copying, enlarging copying and shrinking copying.

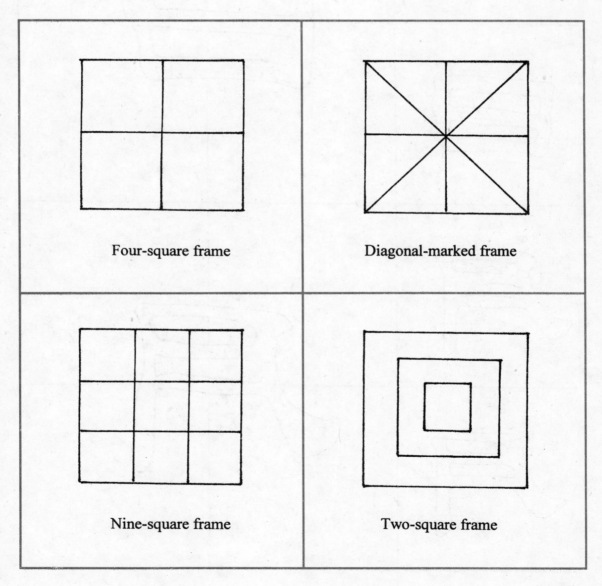

Four-square frame

Diagonal-marked frame

Nine-square frame

Two-square frame

1. Four-Square Frame

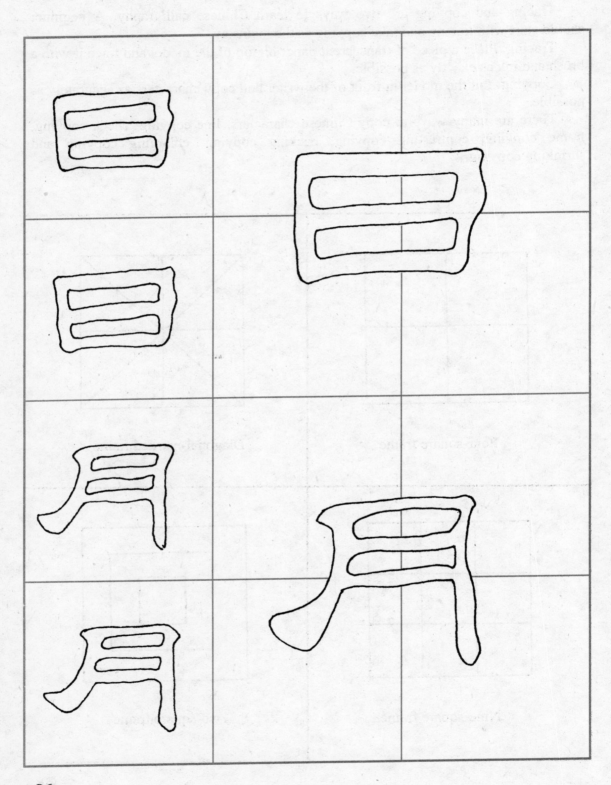

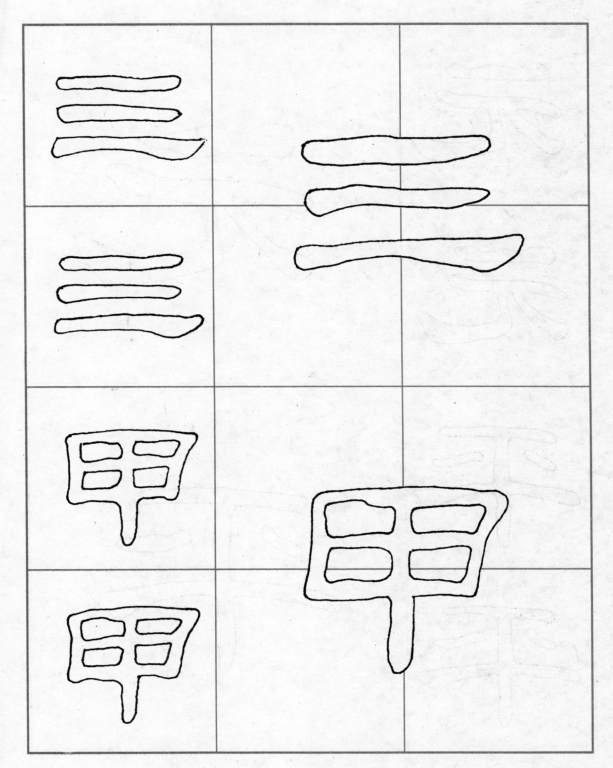

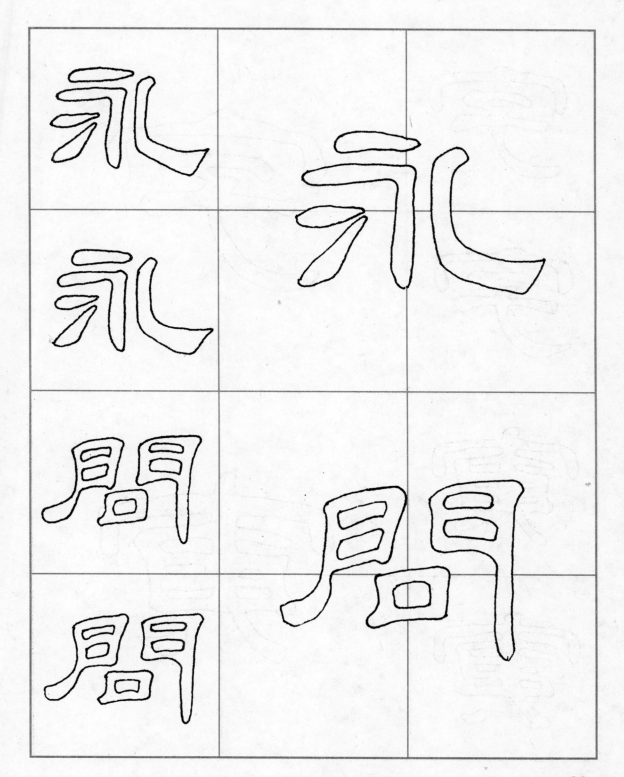

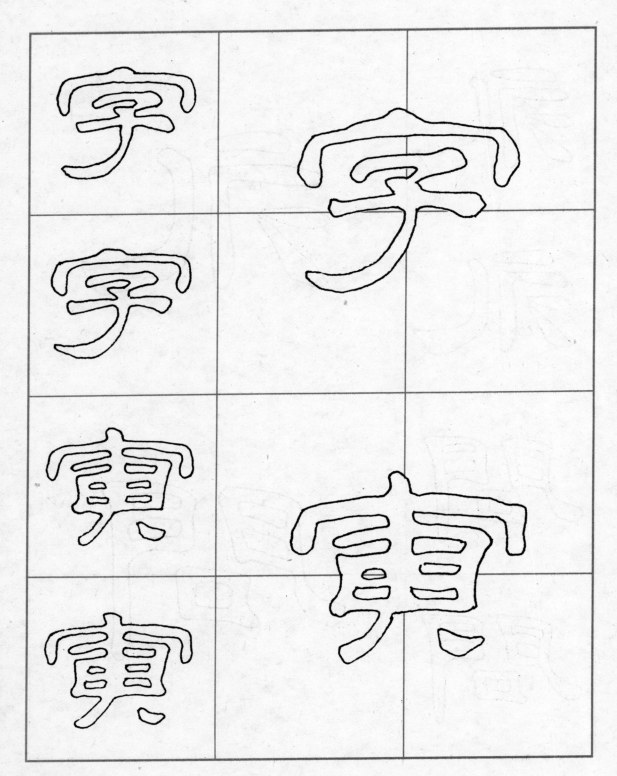

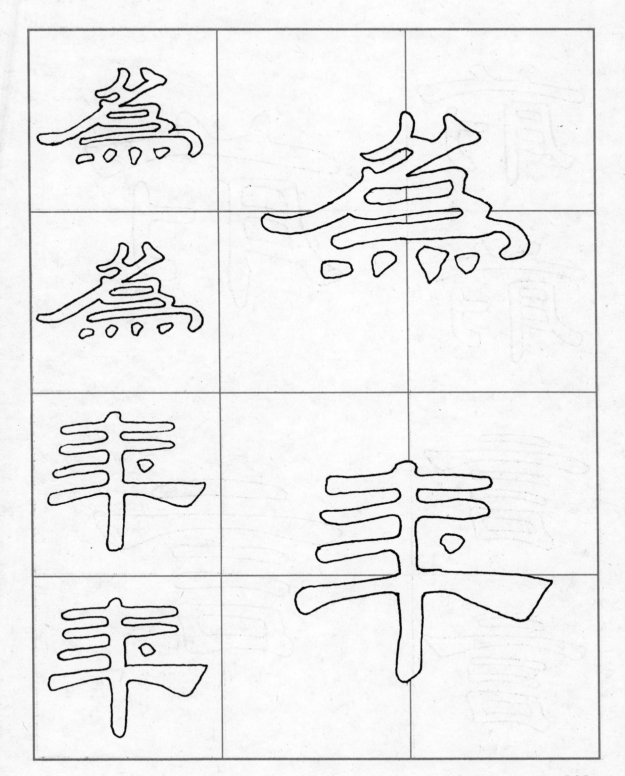

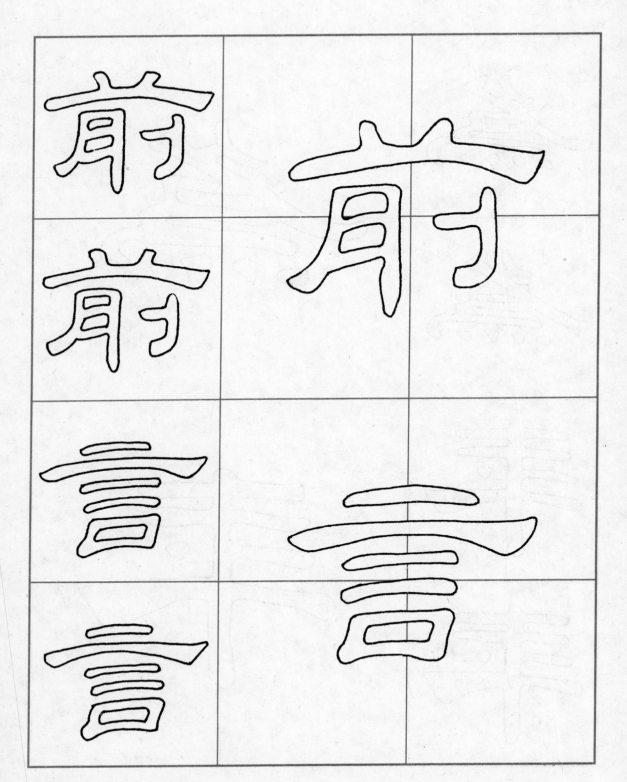

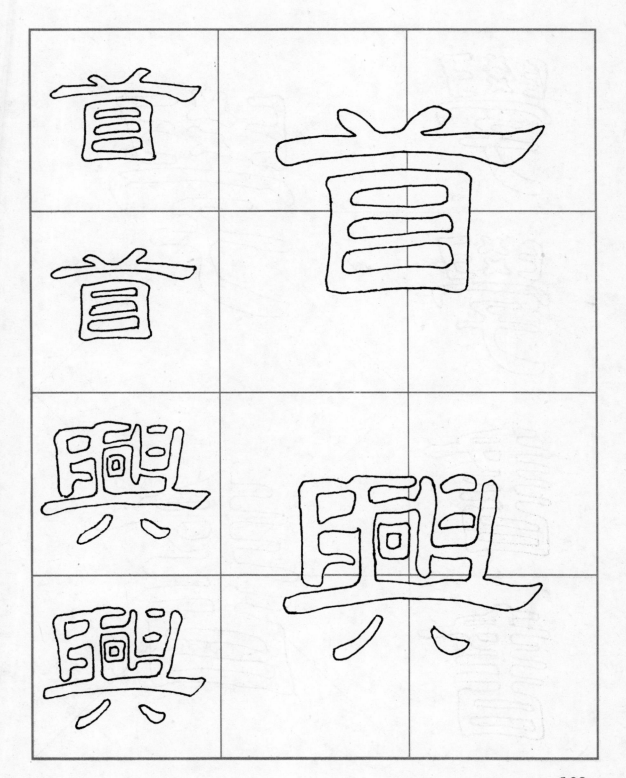

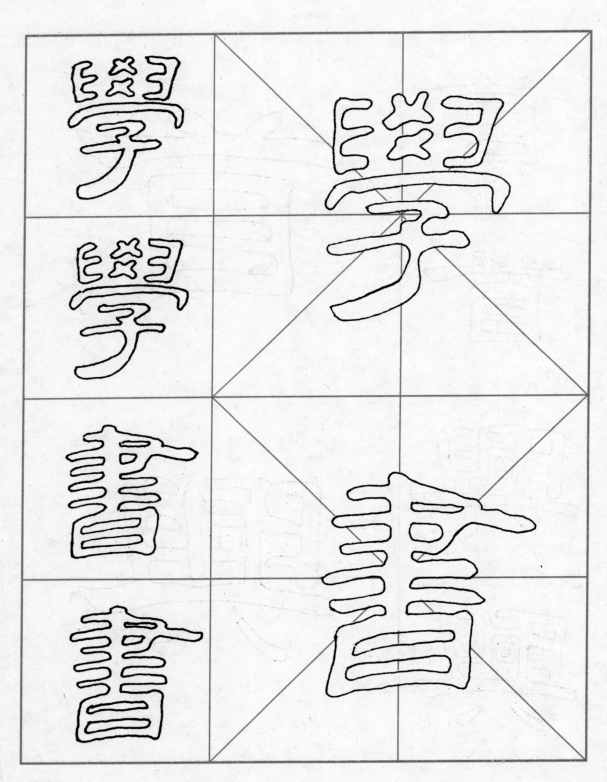

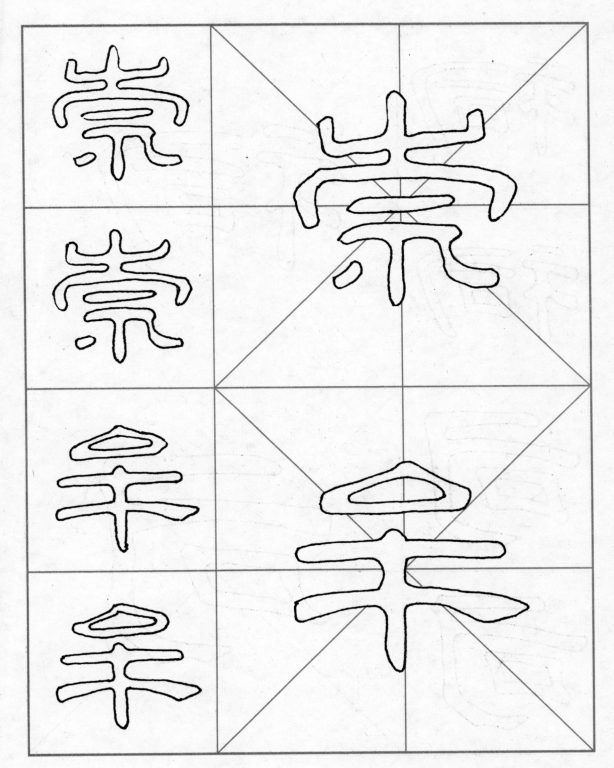

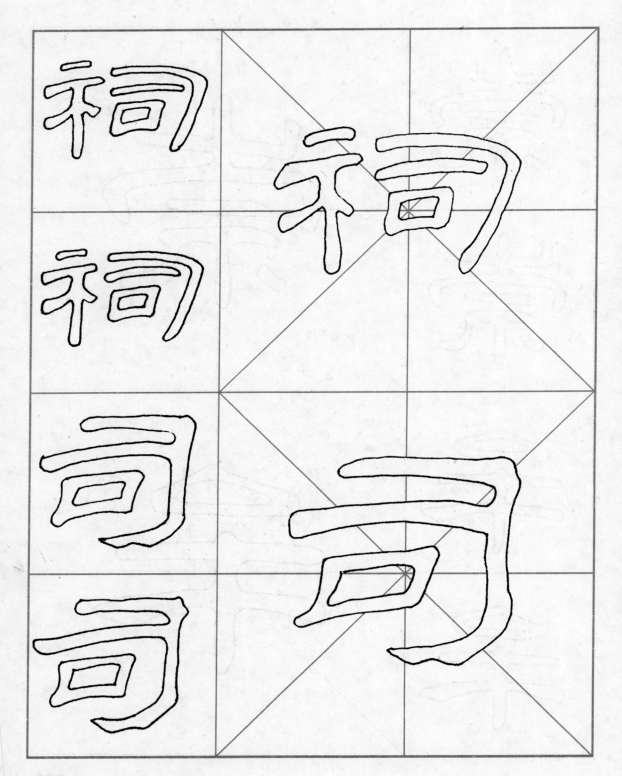

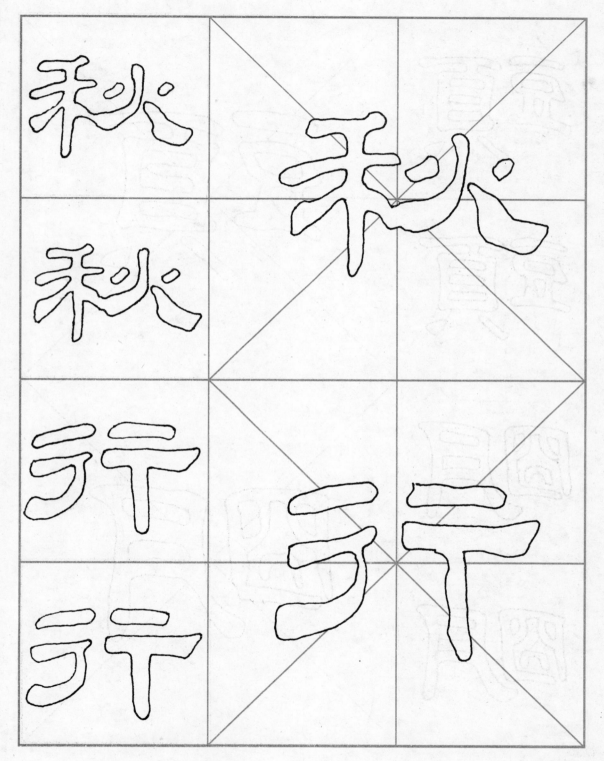

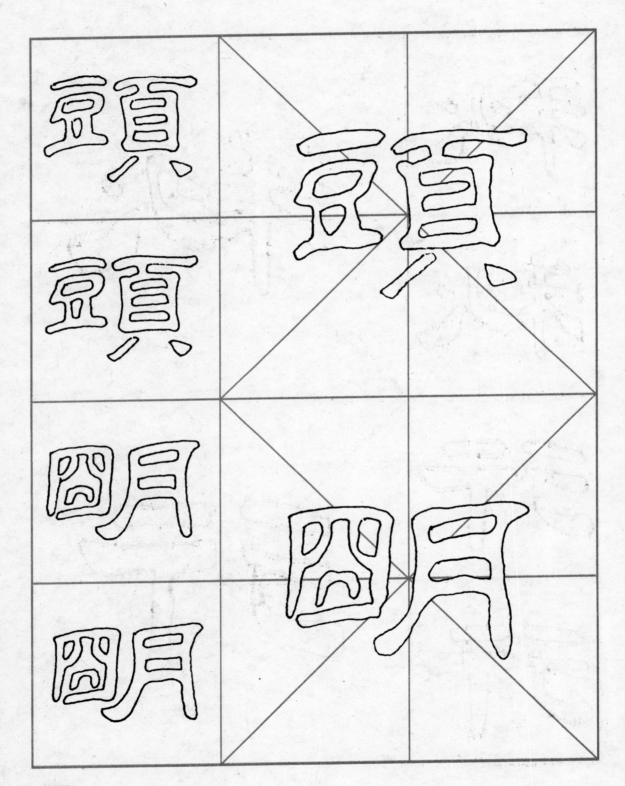

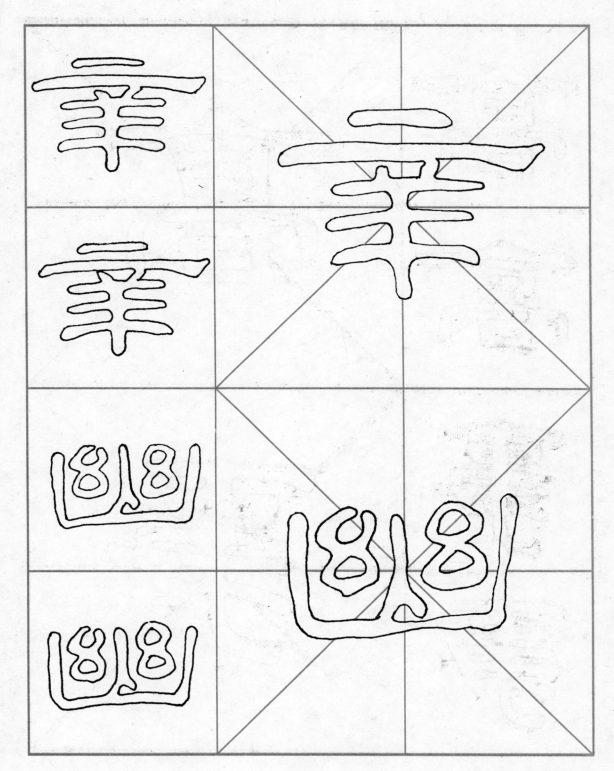

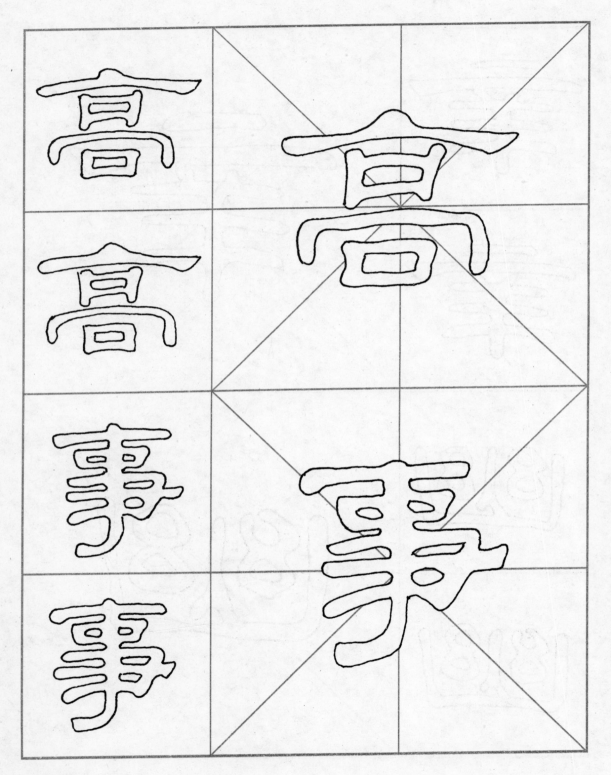

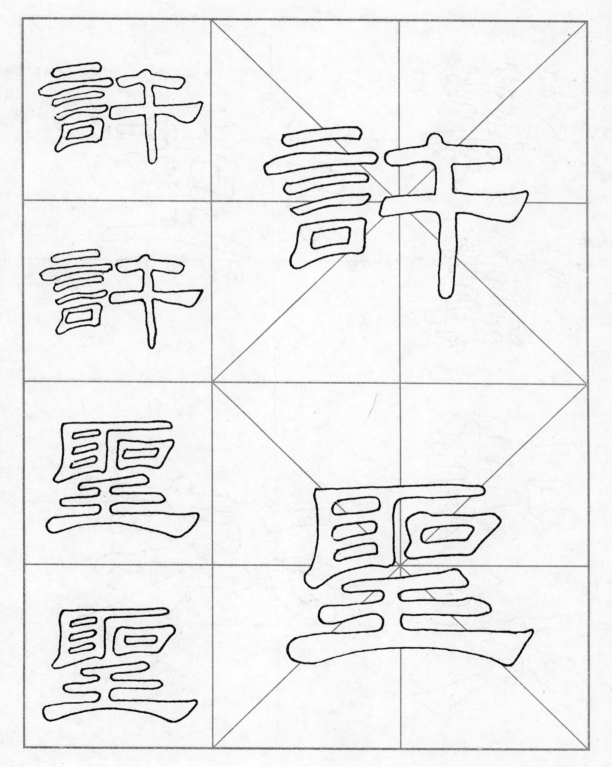

漢 漢

蘯 蘯

徒 徒

徒

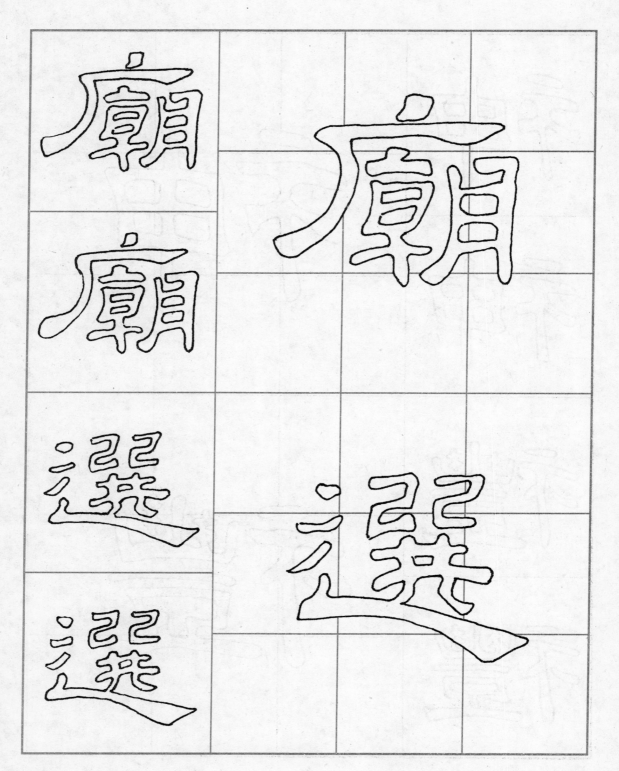

廟

選

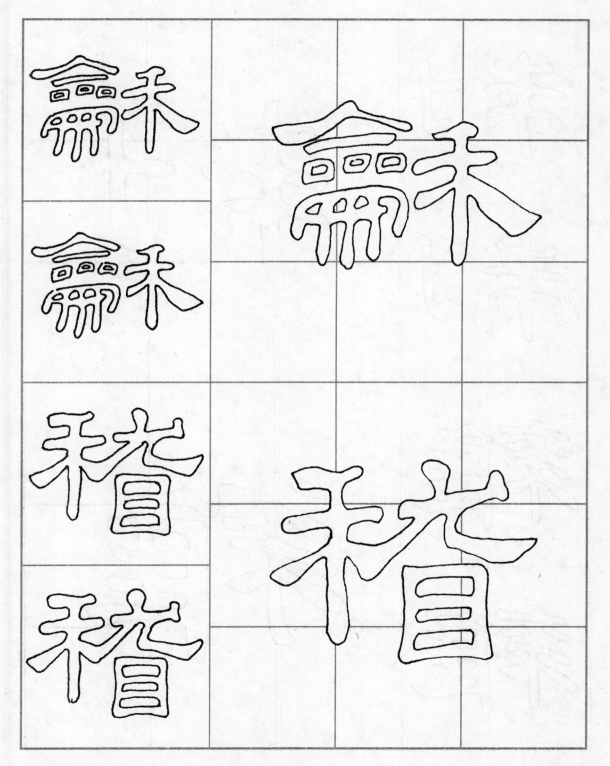

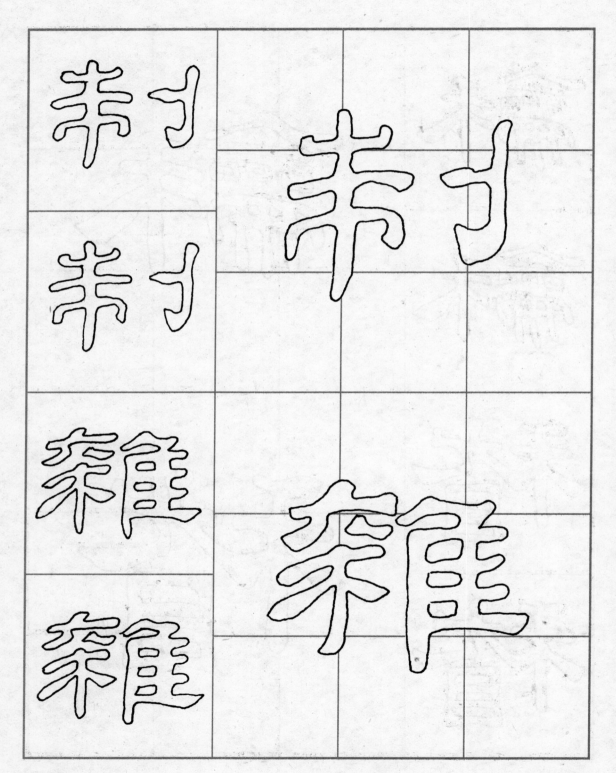

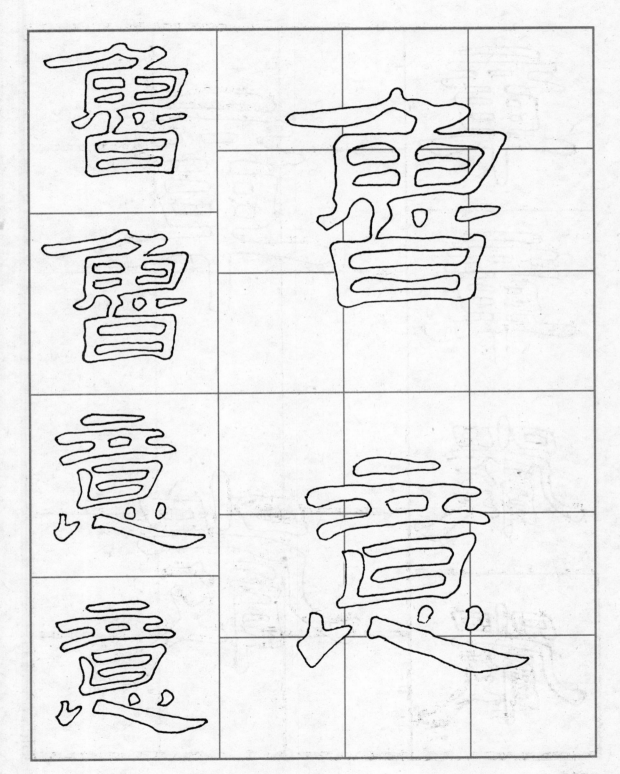

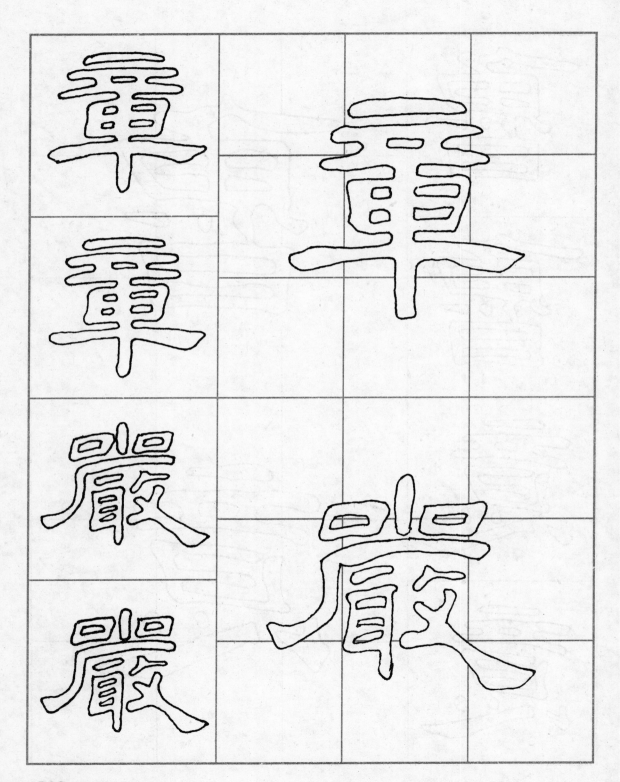

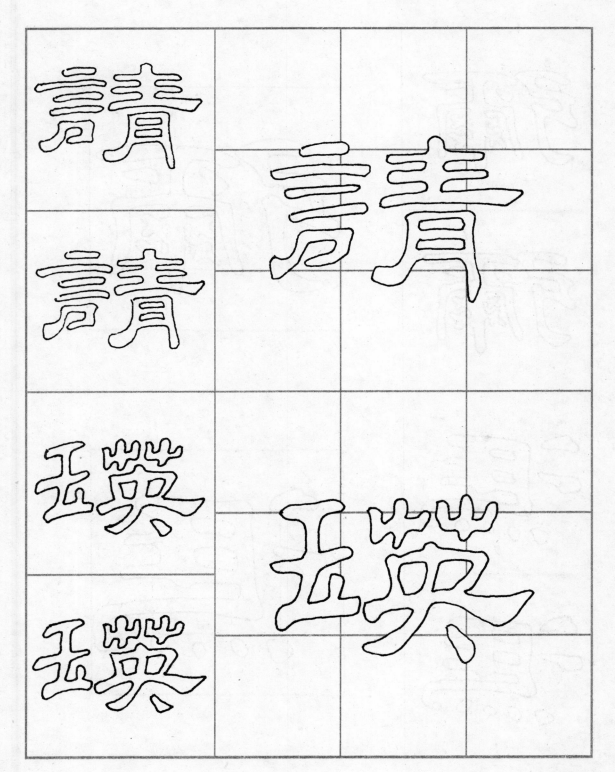

4. Two-Square Frame

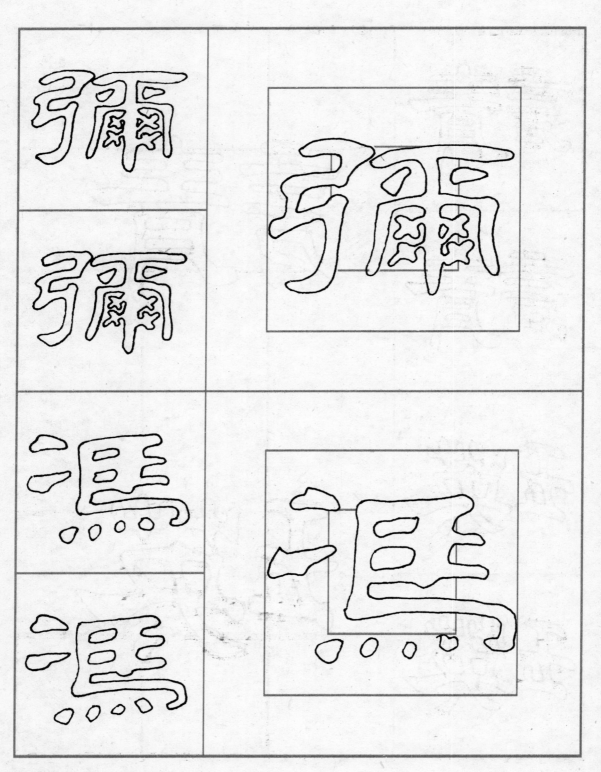

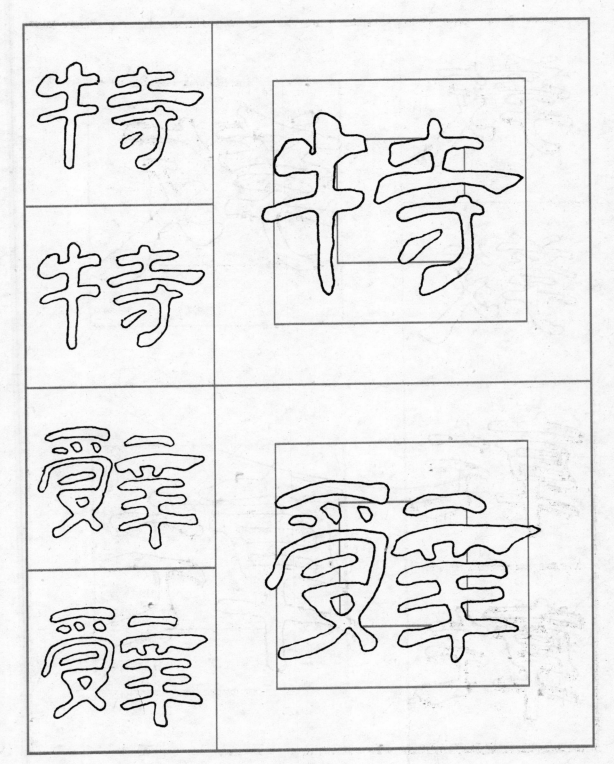

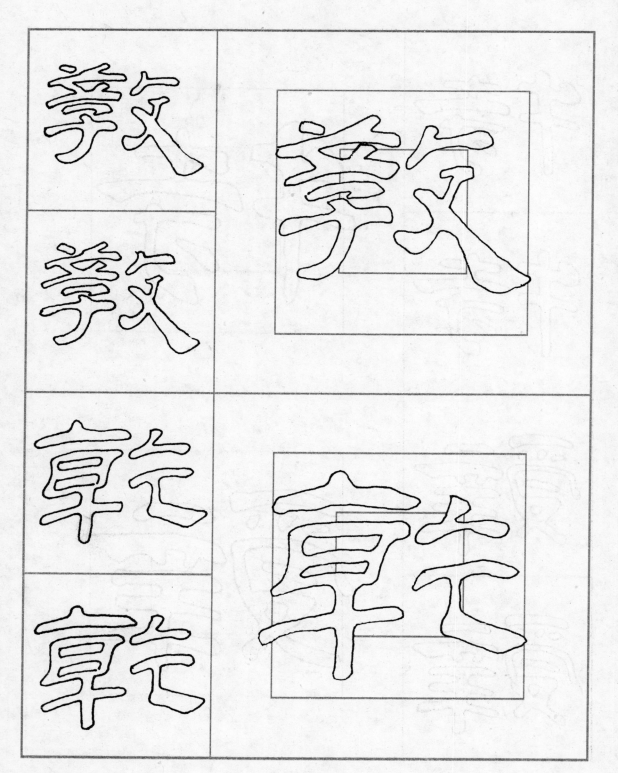

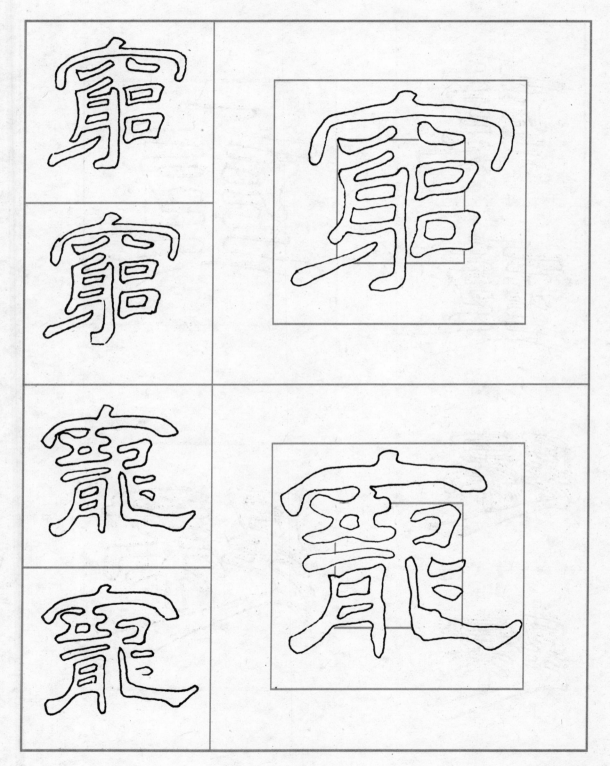

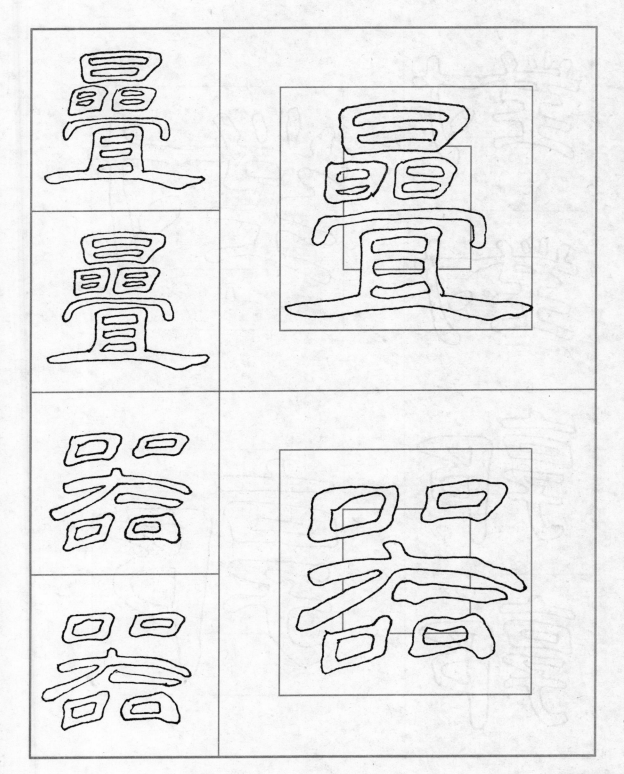

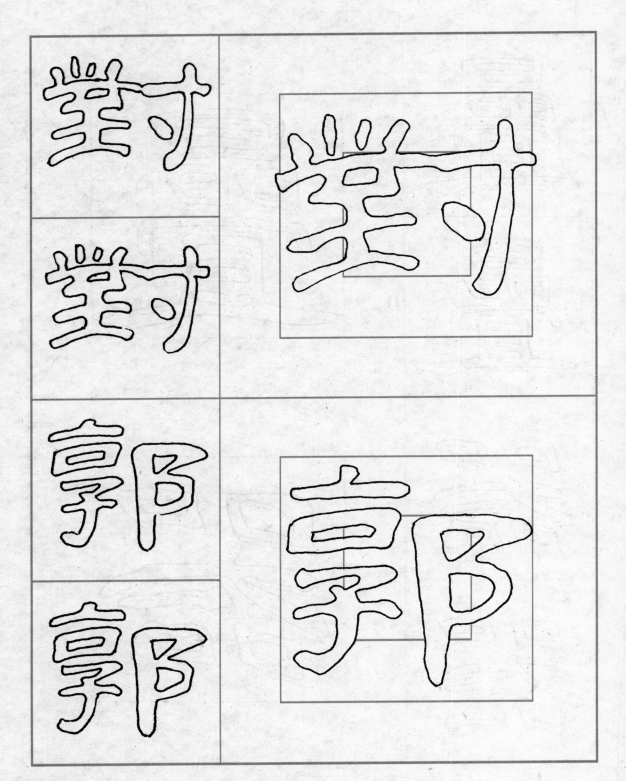

對

對

郭

郭

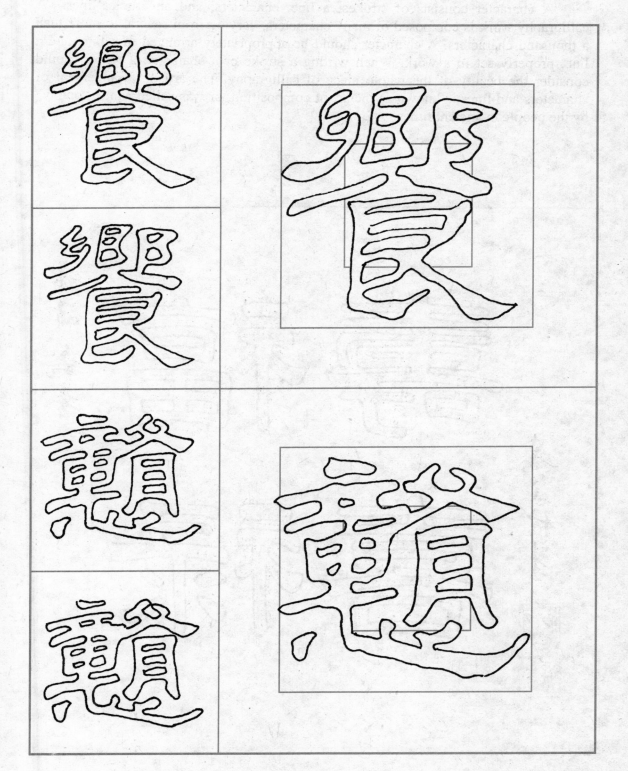

Chapter VII The Art of Composition

"A character consists of strokes; a line, characters; and an article, lines." A calligraphy work is composed of many characters, varying from several to more than a thousand characters. A character should be appropriately arranged in a line, and a line, properly set in a work. When writing a stroke or a character, a writer should consider the beauty of the whole piece of calligraphy. The artistic arrangement of characters and lines is known as the art of composition, or was called as the "outlay" by the people in ancient times.

1. Various Forms of Scrolls

There are various forms of scrolls of Chinese calligraphy, mainly including central scrolls, antithetical couples, vertical-hung, square, horizontal and hand scrolls, albums of calligraphy, round or folding fans, horizontal or vertical inscribed boards and a set of scrolls (mainly consisting of four, six, eight or twelve scrolls). A calligrapher adopts different forms of scrolls of Chinese calligraphy according to the actual needs and his/her appreciation. Different forms of scrolls are arranged in accordance with different arts of composition. A piece of well-written calligraphy and a well-arranged form of scroll may bring out the best in each other.

2. Text

The text is the main part of a work of calligraphy. The following three forms are commonly adopted: a. There are vertical lines and horizontal ranks, all characters arranged in good order. This form is frequently used by the calligraphers creating works of regular, official and small seal scripts. b. There are vertical lines, but not horizontal ranks, making people feel that a well-arranged piece of calligraphy contains some changes. This form is mainly favorable to running script, and to other scripts as well. c. There are neither vertical lines nor horizontal ranks. Completely shaking off all pre-set forms, this form can make a calligrapher feel free to express his/her feelings and create whatever he/she wants. It is mainly suited to large grass character script.

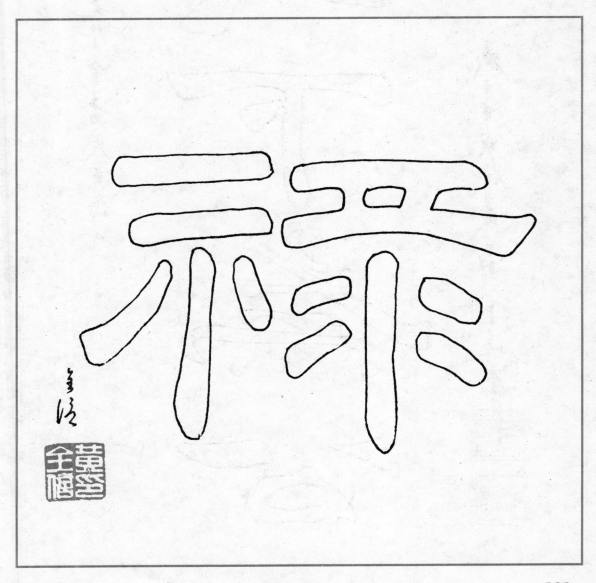

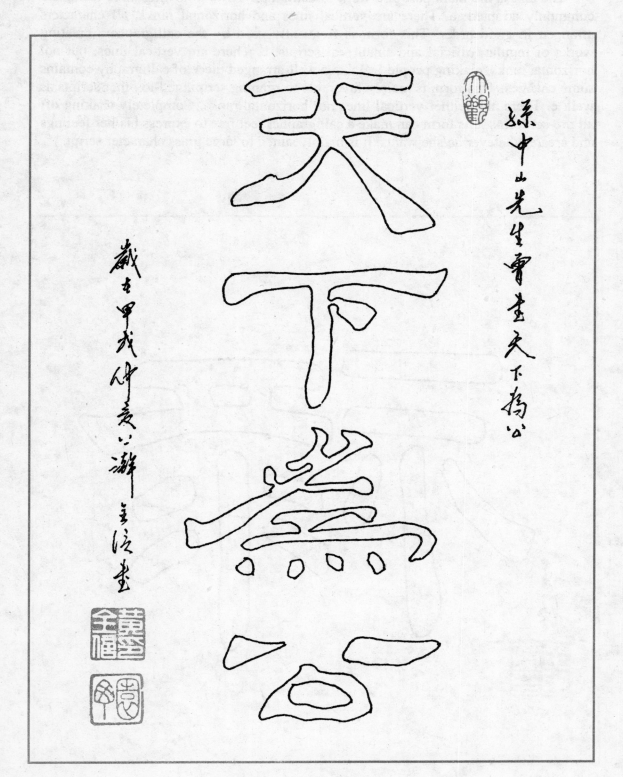

天下為公

孫中山先生曾書天下為公

歲在甲戌仲夏八瀦主法書

3. Inscriptions

The names of recipient and calligrapher are the component parts of a piece of calligraphy. The name of recipient is often written at the top of a calligraphy work; and the name of calligrapher, at the bottom, plus the date and place sometimes. At least, a calligrapher should sign his name at the end of a piece of work. An inscription consisting of many words is called a rich inscription; and an inscription composed of a few words, a poor inscription. The inscription should adopt the same script as or a more cursive script than that of the text, rather than be more neatly written than the text.

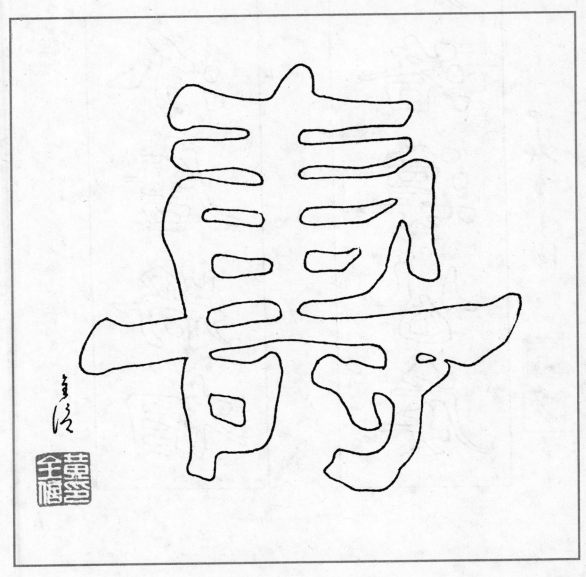

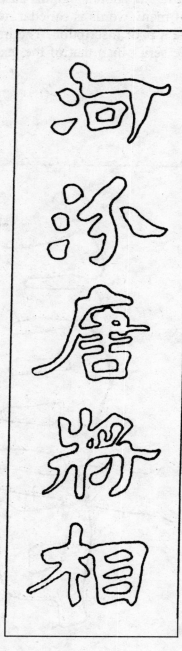

河泳唐粉相

宛洛漢公卿

清楊守敬書聯

甲戌章早清

4. Seals

In general, a seal should be affixed on a piece of calligraphy after the signature. Usually the seal is square in shape and red or white in color. An idle seal showing the calligrapher's refined name, the name of studio or the name of the year may be affixed too. Most of the seals are elliptical. The seal affixed at the beginning of the text is called the head seal; and that affixed at the middle edge of the text, the waist seal. The size, location and style of a seal should match the text and inscription. A red seal adds the touch that brings a work of calligraphy to life.

竹石得幽秉

清程庭鹭刀书联

壶觞多雅游

黄子信书龙泉竹李

Chapter VIII   Creation

The creation of a piece of calligrapher refers to the artistic labor involved in making a calligraphy work. Before the creation of calligraphy work, one is required to have obtained fairly high accomplishments and have a high degree of skill. While creating, one must pour all feelings and thinking into his work to create a splendid space consisting of energetic dots, lines, curving lines, squares, cycles, etc.

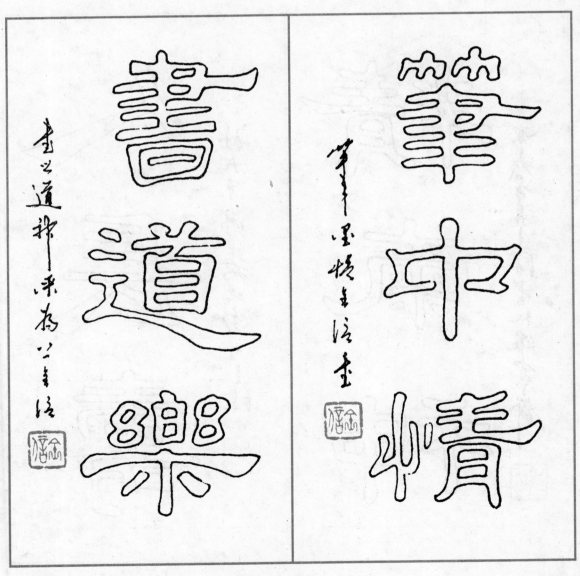

1. Making a Plan Before Writing

Before one starts writing, one should make a well-thought plan concerning the text, inscription, seal, etc., decide how to write characters according to the size of a piece of paper, concentrate one's mind on the brush, spread out the paper prudently and start writing the first stroke resolutely. The profound significance of making a plan is to express the realm that the calligrapher has sought through a concrete calligraphy work. Without a plan, there would be no art. The Chinese calligraphers of the past ages paid great attention to making a plan, believing that the plan plays a leading role in creation.

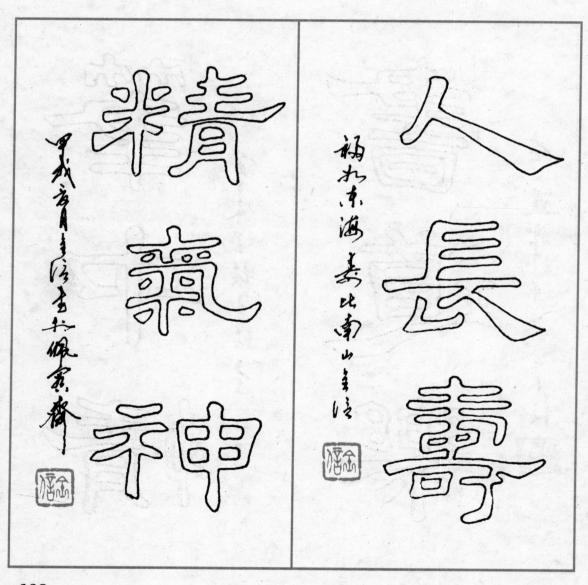

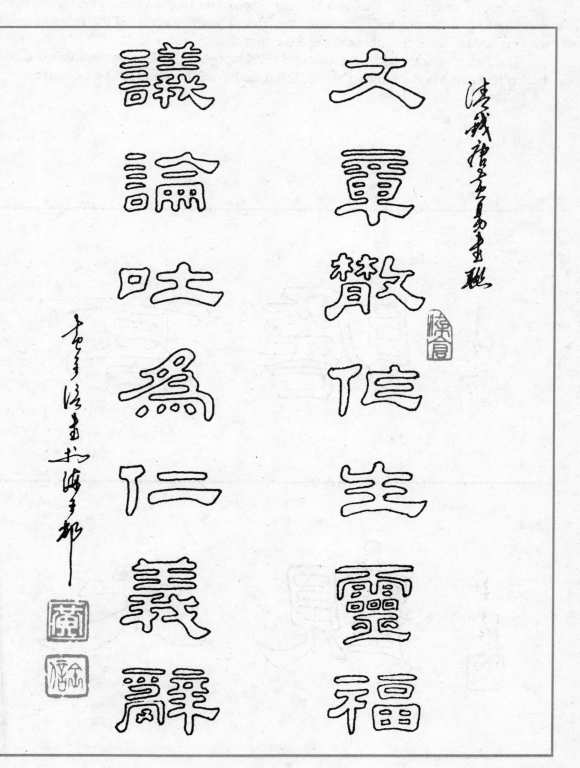

2. The First Character Leads the Whole Text

"The first stroke sets the standards for a character, and the first character leads all characters of an article." This is a brilliant exposition in the *Calligraphy Manual* by Sun Guoting, a famous calligrapher of the Tang Dynasty, stressing the importance of the first stroke in the first character and the first character in a text.

The first character takes the lead of a calligraphy work. Writing the first character well is just like a horse running ahead, followed by ten thousand galloping horses.

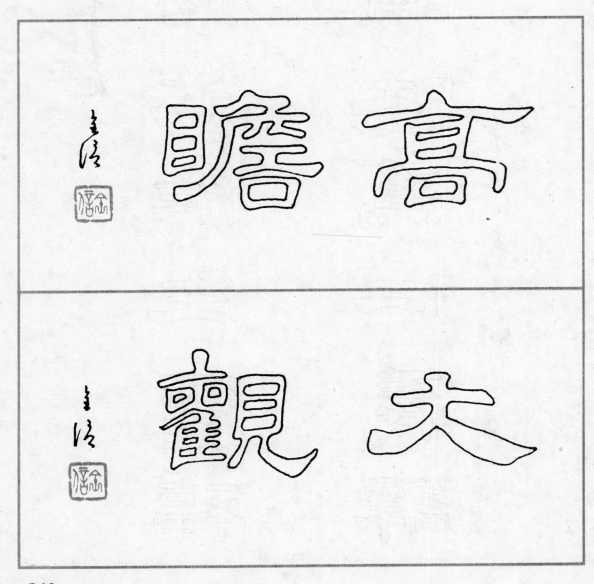

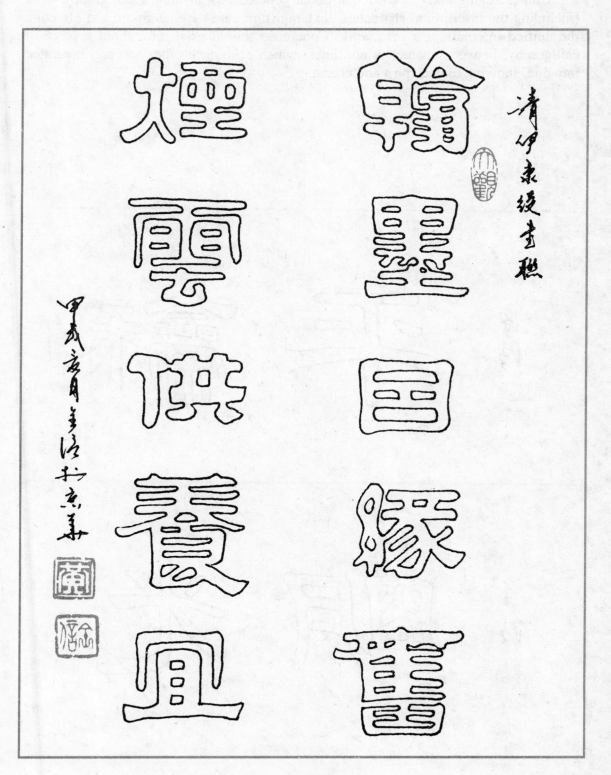

翰墨因緣舊

煙雲供養宜

清伊秉綬書聯

甲戌夏月重臨於東莞

3. A Coherent Whole

Chinese calligraphy is particular about coherence. Finishing a calligraphy work (including the inscription, characters, text, signature, etc.) at one go aims at effecting the unified internal spirit of a work. Coherence should exist throughout a piece of calligraphy, between characters and lines, which echo each other and are integrated into one, showing united spirit and charm.

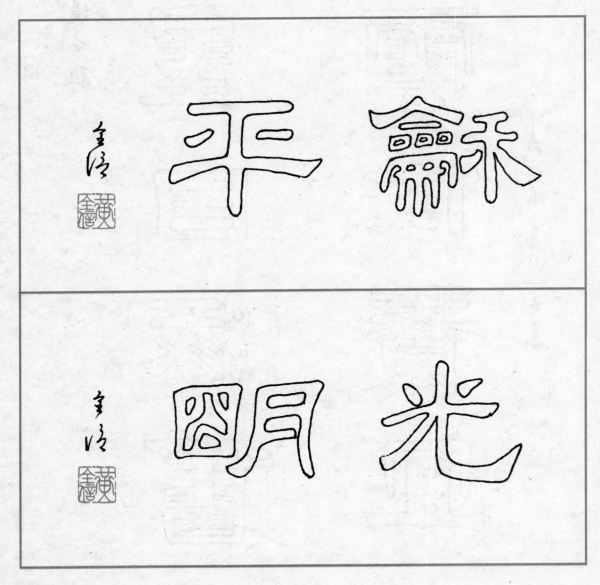

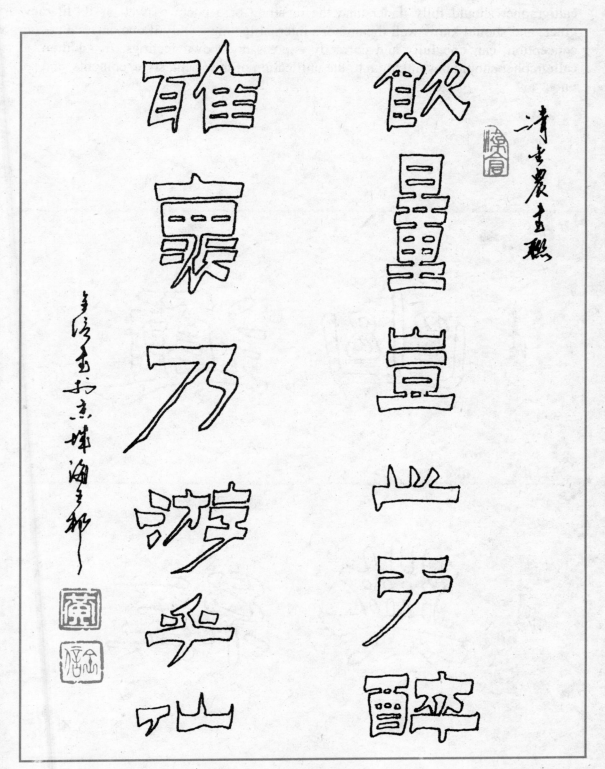

4. A Poetic Conception

"A calligrapher expresses his feelings through his works." Before creation, a calligrapher should fully understand the meaning of a poem as well as its literacy grace, and should know well the author's internal feelings. Only if one enters a poetic conception, can one fully and correctly express one's own feelings. In addition, a calligrapher should pay attention to the unification of the script, style, contents, and so on.

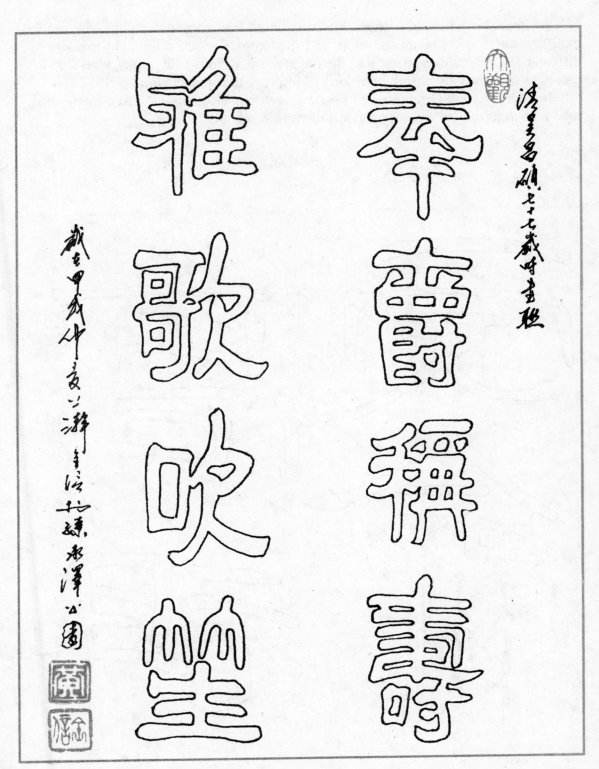

雉歌吹笙

奉壽稱壽

清吳昌碩七十七歲時畫難

歲在甲戌仲夏二游書於北京玉淵潭公園

Chapter IX   Appreciation

To improve the art of calligraphy, one should first copy one calligraphy model until one has a good command of it, and then copy various calligraphy models by different famous calligraphers; and then appreciate various calligraphy works of the past ages to constantly absorb nutrition and improve the appreciation level.

In addition, one is required to read a large number of books, make many trips, read numerous tablets and copy models of various schools.

君諱全字景完敦
煌效穀人也其先
蓋周之胄武王東
乾之楔前伐段

漢曹全碑

蕭金信識

畢務觸石興雲雨
我農桑資糧品物
亦相瑤光崇冠二
州古曰雍梁馮于

漢華山廟碑 歲在甲戌首夕金信識

故經援神

曰宮正制

帝卯行以神

行正以制命

以制神

尚命挈

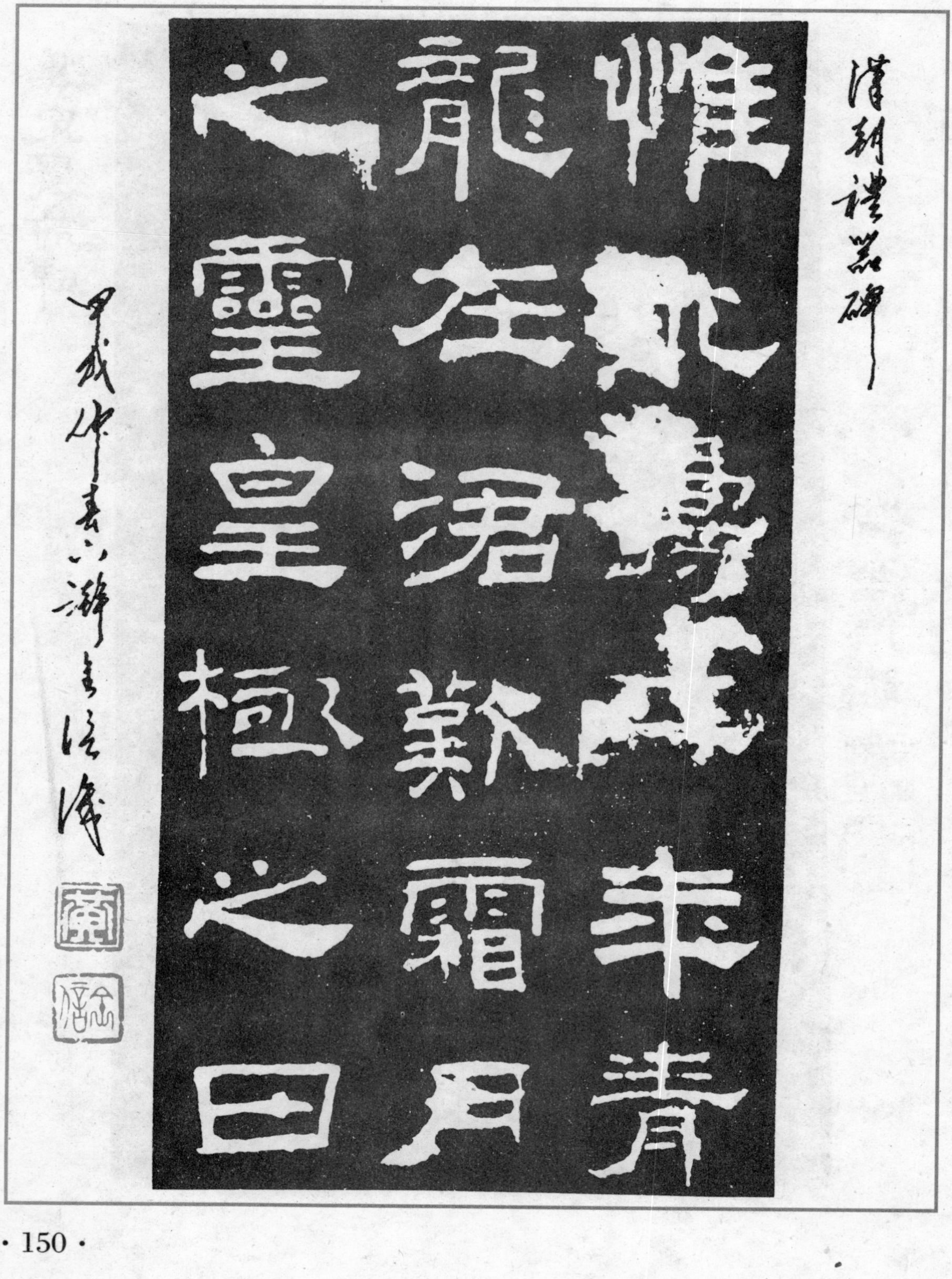

惟北嶽本青

龍左涒歎霜月

之靈皇極之日

清朝禮器碑

甲戌仲春六瀞書於海

司
徒
田

雄
司

空
更
茶

稽
首

言
魯
前

相
瑛

尊卑名帛

考瘟江夫宁

兄瘫門

责任编辑　单　瑛
封面设计　朱　丹　黄全信

图书在版编目（CIP）数据

隶书自学教程 / 黄全信编著。－北京：华语教学出版社，1997.3
（中国书法自学丛书）ISBN 7-80052-455-8

Ⅰ. 隶… Ⅱ. 黄… Ⅲ. 汉字－隶书－自学参考资料 Ⅳ. J292.11

中国版本图书馆 CIP 数据核字（97）第 00816 号

中国书法自学丛书—隶书自学教程

黄全信　编著

*

©华语教学出版社

华语教学出版社出版

（中国北京百万庄路 24 号）

邮政编码　100037

春雷印刷厂印刷

中国国际图书贸易总公司发行

（中国北京车公庄西路 35 号）

北京邮政信箱第 399 号　邮政编码　100044

1998 年（16 开）第一版

（汉英）

ISBN 7-80052-455-8 / H · 547（外）

03500

9 － CE － 3193P